Have you ever felt like a nonperson?

Too often our sense of personal worth is wounded by subtle "messages," both real and imagined, from the world around us. The result is a negative self-image that is far removed from what we believe about God's love. Now a program is available to help you change these feelings of inadequacy into renewed confidence. Verna Birkey offers positive alternatives by focusing your attention on God's loving design for your life. More than a thoughtful study of biblical truth, YOU ARE VERY SPECIAL maps out a specific course of action you can take to begin a truly transformed lifestyle. Let the author help you redefine your individual value as a unique creation of God.

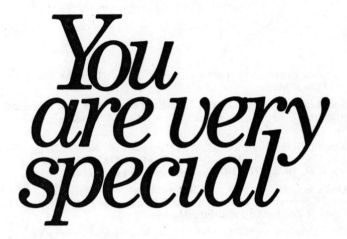

You
are very
special

Verna Birkey

Fleming H. Revell Company
Tarrytown, New York

Scripture quotations not otherwise identified are from the King James Version of the Bible.

Scripture quotations identified AMPLIFIED are from The Amplified New Testament, © The Lockman Foundation 1954, 1958, and are used by permission.

Scripture quotations identified NAS are from the New American Standard Bible, Copyright © THE LOCKMAN FOUNDATION 1960, 1962, 1963, 1968, 1971, 1972, 1973, 1975 and are used by permission.

Quotations from GREAT VERSES THROUGH THE BIBLE, by F. B. Meyer. Copyright © 1966 by Marshall, Morgan and Scott Ltd. Used by permission of Zondervan Publishing House.

For information on the Enriched Living Workshops taught by Verna Birkey, write: Seminar Workshops for Women, P.O. Box 3039, Kent, WA. 98031.

Library of Congress Cataloging in Publication Data

Birkey, Verna.
    You are very special.

    1. Women—Religious life.   2. Bible—Meditations.
3. Self-respect.   I. Title.
BV4527.B57   248'.843   77-23805
ISBN 0-8007-5032-2

Contents

TO my dear parents, whose influence, prayers, training, and example have made a profound impression on my life, and who have faithfully communicated their love and God's love to me

I am deeply grateful...

TO my dear friend and assistant, Jeanette Turnquist—"Nettie," for working closely with me through each chapter and giving wise and perceptive suggestions and contributions.

TO two other dear friends and co-workers— Doris Swain, for her diligent and patient typing and retyping of the manuscript, and Carol Longston, for her ready help and valuable assistance in research and typing.

TO my faithful staff and dear friends for their help, encouragement, and especially prayer for me during the writing.

TO the thousands of Enriched Living Workshop alumnae who have graciously and thoughtfully shared their experiences, questions, feelings, and thoughts.

Introduction

In my contacts with people, I have found so many dear women who find it difficult to really believe that God loves them with an unconditional, unchanging love. They find it difficult to believe they are important, persons of worth, of value. They entertain negative, uncomfortable thoughts about themselves and inwardly question God's care and concern for them.

The Lord asserts that He wants His people to be a joyful, trusting, comfortable people. In Isaiah 40:1 He says, "Comfort ye, comfort ye my people . . . ." He goes on to indicate that this comfort comes through *knowing who He is* and *knowing who we really are* and results in deeper confidence in Him.

One's sense of personal worth, or lack of it, is influenced by "messages" from parents, teachers, friends that have been received and believed. We tend to feel about ourselves as we *think* others feel about us. And the tendency is to think that the way *others* feel about us is the way *God* feels about us.

Many women who attended the Enriched Living Workshop have shared with me the new joy and peace they have found as they have begun to really bask in God's love and goodness. They have experienced a new and proper love for themselves as they have basked in the truths expressed in the song "God Has Made Me

9

Very Special" and allowed God to write this indelibly upon their hearts.

Most of the time when we're discouraged, anxious, frustrated, worried, joyless, it's because we have failed to remember who we are and who He is. We aren't, at that moment, really believing Him. We aren't agreeing with Him when He tells us who we are.

The message in this book is designed to help you realize in fresh, vivid ways who you really are, who He is, and what He promises to be to each of us. Our problem is not so much that we haven't heard the truth, but that we haven't considered what it really means, or we do not really believe what it says. If we did, we would experience so much less worry, fear, frustration in feeling of no value, no worth, useless.

My desire then in sharing this book with you is to give a practical, workable plan to help us actually believe what God says about us and about Himself. God, in His Word, gives us clear statements of fact, but we benefit from these truths only as we really believe what God says. We must agree with Him and bring every fiber of our being, every straying or contrary thought, and take it captive and make it obey Him, agree with Him, believe Him. Then, and only then, will we feel good about ourselves and Him and experience the inner comfort and confidence that He wants us to have.

The purpose of this book is not simply to give you something to read through and put on the shelf. It is designed for your meditation, study, and action. It is, in a sense, a program of belief—an aid to help you know and believe that you are someone very special and that God is all He claims to be.

The song on page 15, "God Has Made Me Very Special," has been planned to help you fill your mind and heart with the truths presented throughout this book. If you can, memorize it and sing it often. At the end of each chapter you will find "Turning Insight Into Action." These are projects designed to, first of all, make the truths of each chapter real in your own life and, secondly, to help you demonstrate the truth to others. As you delve into the Scripture, memorize verses, and do some practical, thoughtful things for others, you will find your own sense of worth (as well as theirs) growing.

Dear friend, I pray that the following assertions of how good God is, how lovingly He feels toward you, and what He promises to do for you and to make of you will encourage you and challenge you to rise to the occasion of faith every time. Bask in these precious truths. Take the comfort of them and let God communicate to your heart that indeed you *are* someone very special. In doing this you will develop a proper sense of self-worth as viewed from God's perspective.

Ways You Can Use This Book

This book is a program of belief. It has been designed to lead you into the comfort of a sure knowledge that you are very special and that God is who He says He is. Each chapter ends with "Turning Insight Into Action" to help you get the truths worked out in daily believing and living.

There are many ways you can read and use this book:

Read it straight through to get the total message.

Read and concentrate on one chapter, memorizing and meditating on that one truth for at least a week.

Read it and work on "Turning Insight Into Action" with one other person—friend, husband, wife, child, pupil, and so forth.

Read it with your family. Work together on "Turning Insight Into Action."

Use it in small group studies—Sunday-school classes, home Bible-study groups, campus groups, and other special groups.

It should be read with a pen and ruler. Underline statements that speak to your own need. Note in the margin any ideas that expand the truth or relate it to your

previous experience or knowledge. Read it with your
Bible at hand. Look up the Scriptures; mark them in
your Bible.

Thousands of women have found that the basic principle given in this book really works—that meditating on
who God is and what He thinks of me brings inner peace
and comfort. "Thou wilt keep him in perfect peace,
whose mind is stayed on thee: because he trusteth in
thee" (Isaiah 26:3).

God Has Made Me Very Special

(Tune: Guide Me, O
Thou Great Jehovah)

Verna Birkey

John Hughes

1. God has made me ver-y spe-cial And I'm dear-ly
2. I am still a per-son in pro-cess, Work-man-ship of
3. I'm of val-ue made u-nique-ly, With a pur-pose
4. I'm so weak, but He sus-tains me, Gives me strength for
5. Since I'm now com-mit-ted to Him, He's re-spon-si-
6. I am God's own spe-cial trea-sure, One who's pre-cious

loved by Him E-ven though He knows me ful-ly,
God's own hand. E-ven though so deep-ly fall-en,
that's di-vine. God has giv-en an as-sign-ment
eve-ry day. My Com-pan-ion ev-ery mo-ment,
ble for me. I am un-der His pro-tec-tion,
in His sight. He has set His love up-on me

He ac-cepts me as I am. How I praise Him, how I praise Him,
I'm re-deemed by His great grace. How I praise Him, how I praise Him,
To bring glo-ry to His Name. How I praise Him, how I praise Him,
He is with me all the way. How I praise Him, how I praise Him,
Ob-ject of His con-stant care. How I praise Him, how I praise Him,
And in Him my soul de-lights. Oh, what won-der, how a-maz-ing!

For His won-drous love for me, For His won-drous love for me.
For His won-drous grace to me, For His won-drous grace to me.
Called to glo-ri-fy His Name, Called to glo-ri-fy His Name.
For His pre-sence and His strength, For His pre-sence and His strength.
For His con-stant, lov-ing care, For His con-stant, lov-ing care.
He has set His love on me, He has set His love on me.

1

You Are Someone Very Special

"I'll never find a friend more special than you . . . ."
"For my special friend . . . ."
"It takes all kinds, but your kind is the nicest!"
"With special thoughts of you."
"Merry Christmas to a very special friend."
These are words we all love to hear. Whether the message is spoken or scribbled or lettered on parchment or shown through a little deed or look, we love to have people communicate to us how very special we are to them.

Do you know that you are someone very special? God thinks you are. You are a very special person to Him—"the apple of His eye," the object of His love.

I talked recently with one who had made this exciting discovery. She spoke of the many ways God had shown her how special she is to Him.

. . . His preserving and protecting power over me these many years, His providing me with a loving family, His providing spiritual blessings innumerable—fellowship with other Christians, His Word, and most of all, salvation through His Son, Jesus Christ. He has lovingly provided my needs. Even His leading me to attend the Enriched Living Workshop spoke to me of my "specialness" to Him. Since the Workshop, I don't just look back at the so-called "good" things as examples of His love for me, but I now see my whole life, all that has occurred, every minute detail, as part of His love for me. Now as things occur daily I can see each one as a way of God telling me that I am special, because no one else has the same details in her life as I do. It's as though He says, "Emily, I planned the details of today just for you—to show you that you are My own special treasure!"

Read what God thinks of His very own people, of you, His very own child. *You are His own special treasure.* ". . . you shall be My own possession [my own special treasure] among all the peoples, for all the earth is Mine" (Exodus 19:5 NAS). You are very special by creation. God created you in His own image (*see* Genesis 1:27). He created you for His glory. ". . . I have created him for my glory, I have formed him; yea, I have made him" (Isaiah 43:7).

The loving Heavenly Father created you, formed you, redeemed you, called you by your name, and claims you as His very own.

But now thus saith the Lord that created thee, O Jacob, and he that formed thee, O Israel, Fear not: for I have redeemed thee, I have called thee by thy name; thou art mine.

Isaiah 43:1

You are one in whom "His soul delights" (*see* Isaiah 42:1). He keeps you as the "apple of His eye" (*see* Deuteronomy 32:10). You are very precious in His sight (*see* Isaiah 43:4).

At first you might think these precious words apply only to Jacob and Israel, God's people in the Old Testament. But listen to what He says in the New Testament: "But ye are a chosen generation, a royal priesthood, an holy nation, a peculiar people . . ." (1 Peter 2:9). In other words, all of these titles now belong to you who are God's redeemed children.

In these and so many other places in the Scriptures, God tells you that you are very special to Him. He wants to be your God, and He wants you to know that you are His person.

Continually Recording Messages

So often our perception of God's loving thoughts toward us is colored by the love or lack of love communicated to us through the years by those closest to us. Emily's exciting discovery of her specialness to God was no doubt strongly influenced by the love of her wise and thoughtful parents.

> They were always so proud of all my achievements and let me know it. My mother used to say how happy my brothers and I made her. She always said that she would enjoy raising us all over again, because we were such a pleasure to her. It truly made me feel that I was someone very special to them.

You may not feel that you are very special to God, to your parents, or to anyone. Your thoughts may be totally opposite. You may have been thinking that you don't have a great personality or special looks or even special abilities. How could you possibly be *special?* How could you be a person of value, of worth?

Your feelings, your thoughts are not an accurate measure of the true situation. All of us are continually recording messages—negative messages or positive messages. The positive messages affirm our worth as a person and bring encouragement and a sense of adequacy. "Honey, if *you* did it, I know it was done right!" The negative messages deny our worth and bring discouragement, a sense of insecurity and inadequacy. "No one will ever want to marry *you!*"

Quite in contrast to Emily's experience of loving, affirming parents was Annette's sharing her response and feelings as a result of her parents continually criticizing her.

> I accepted Christ into my life when I was seventeen years old. As time passed, something seemed to be missing. Very dissatisfied with myself, depressed, pessimistic—I blamed it all on my critical parents. I lowered my standards, gave up my Christian profession, and even went so far as to leave my husband and children. I had had nothing to do with God, and now I had nothing to hold on to. Of course, the whole situation was more than I could take, and I found myself crying out to God for help. I truly repented of my sin—being such a selfish person. It was really a miracle, because God did hear me, forgive me, and bring me back to Himself. Oh, what a great, loving, compassionate, long-suffering Father He has been! I must surely be someone very special to have the privilege of knowing Him and to have such fellowship with Him through His Word.

We tend to feel of worth or of no worth according to how we *think* other people feel toward us. From infancy and early childhood we have been recording these positive and negative messages. If parents are cold and matter-of-fact, unable or unwilling to express affection, the child concludes that he is unlovely, unlovable. One shared, "Whenever I would put my arms around my father and say 'I love you,' out of awkwardness he would take my arms down and push me away. It made me feel so alone and unwanted."

If parents react out of impatience with the child's slow learning of skills or habits, the child will feel he is a bother and think he is very inadequate. If the parent is irritated over the baby's middle-of-the-night needs or the child's slow learning of motor skills, the child will record negative messages about himself in response to these negative attitudes.

An infant, a child, even an older person tends to feel he is the cause of the negative reactions in the parent, the teacher, the friend, the husband. He then concludes he is a bother, not pleasing, and doubts his worth, feels anxious, frustrated, and insecure.

A censoring voice tone, a condescending manner, a disapproving facial expression, harsh, critical, over-exaggerated words easily cause the child to feel inse-cure, inadequate, unloved, of no worth. As he grows older he continues to confirm and enlarge this negative mental picture of himself. With this negative frame of reference rather solidly imbedded, he continues to pick up on negative messages about himself. In this climate his negative thoughts about himself thrive. He tends to so easily misinterpret the actions and feelings of others toward him in the light of this negative mental picture. He infers that others also have these negative thoughts about him and that even God thinks of him in this way.

Even when someone says an affirming, encouraging word, he tends to overlook it or diminish its value, be-cause he already has such a strong negative focus and a deep persuasion of being of no value, no worth. He be-comes according to his mental picture of himself. He believes the negative thoughts. "For as he thinketh in his heart. so is he . . ." (Proverbs 23:7).

Accept God's Viewpoint

If you identify with those feelings, those thoughts of inadequacy, you really don't feel very special. You may not understand how you could ever be very special to anyone, not even the Lord. If you feel this way, it will be very, very important that you see who you really are—that you're someone very special from God's viewpoint. Accept this truth from Him and begin to agree with Him regardless of your former thoughts or feelings. Repeat to yourself again and again these precious truths. Pause often to thank the Lord that these words from His Word are true and do express how He feels toward you. Verbally thank Him, using these specific words of Scripture. Gradually you will begin to believe that you really are "God's own special treasure, one who's precious in His sight"—truly a person of value, of worth.

O Blessed Lord, how You can take me to be Your own special treasure is beyond my understanding. What wonder, how amazing! Yet because You have said it, I know it is true. I must not look back on my past failures, or even in upon my present weaknesses or unworthiness, but only out, away, up to You and to Your great mercy and love. I will ever praise You for setting Your love upon me and choosing me as Your own. Thank You for letting me be one of Your special people and for being my God. You have given Yourself to me! What more could I ask? You are the strength of my heart and my portion forever. In Jesus' name, amen.

Turning Insight Into Action

1. Expand Your Understanding

From the following verses write down all the special names or descriptions God gives to His people. Check several versions and notice the marginal notations.

GOD HAS SAID

>"The Lord thy God hath chosen thee
to be a special people unto himself"
(Deuteronomy 7:6).

THEREFORE I MAY BOLDLY SAY

*I am
someone
very special.*

Deuteronomy 7:6–8
Exodus 19:3–6
1 Peter 2:9, 10

Circle one of the names or descriptions which especially tells you that you are very special to God. (Note: Even though these words in Exodus and Deuteronomy were written to "Jacob" and "Israel," 1 Peter indicates that all of these old titles for God's people now belong to His children today.)

2. Search and Share

In what ways is God continually indicating to you that you are special? Refer back to the chapter, reread Scripture references, and use the illustration below.

Quite often I encounter others who seem to do things better than I can. Even during my school days I could never be *best* in anything. Someone always did it better. But over and over God has restored confidence in me by putting someone in my path, soon after those feelings occur, to whom I can be a help. Each time He shows me something special I can do for Him. Instead of concentrating on the things I can't do as well as others, I have learned to congratulate them, be glad for them, and concentrate on developing the skills which are peculiar to me.

3. Develop Your Awareness

During this coming week write down three times when you become aware that you are very special to God. Perhaps He will help you in a difficult situation, give adequate physical energy, remind you of something important, or aid you in some other way.

Write down several positive messages that have come to you through others, expressing—you're okay, you're of worth, you're special. Or form some positive messages you can give to others.

4. *Store Up God's Thoughts*

"The Lord thy God hath chosen thee to be a special people unto himself" (Deuteronomy 7:6).

Alternate verse—1 Peter 2:9.

5. *Reach Out in Love*

This week make a special effort to let at least one person know that he is very special to you. Possible love actions:

(a) Create a *hello* card for a grandparent. Involve the whole family if possible. Each could cut a picture from a magazine which brings memories of happy times with the grandparent. Paste the pictures on a paper and write a few comments on each to make the card meaningful. Buy an unusual stamp and mail the *custom-made* card.

(b) Include a single person in your plans this week. Invite him or her to be with your family at a family-oriented church activity, to your home to have dinner with you or your family, or for an evening of fun and games, to go out to lunch with you, or to go shopping and have tea at a mall. You could be a means of encouragement to another. Here's one single person's experience:

At my church I am the only single person my age. Therefore, I do not really fit in any Sunday-school class. What a good feeling this past Sunday to be approached by a married lady with two small children, inviting me to share with her Sunday-school class potluck supper. How good to be included in something other than being asked to teach a class. I love to teach, and it's very rewarding, but it was the feeling of being included in a social sense that was uplifting!

(c) Play a game with or read a story to a younger brother or sister.

(d) Create a special name for someone you love. Let it be a means of conveying encouragement and love. It need not become a regular name, but just used occasionally to convey the special message, "You're okay." Make sure the other person knows what you mean when you call him that name. One husband called his wife "Beautiful!" She shared her reaction:

> I don't see myself as a beauty, but my husband sure does. In fact he calls me Beautiful more than he does Brenda. The names we call people are tremendously important. Every time he says Beautiful I feel like a queen, and he treats me like one!

(e) Spend time with someone else (husband, wife, child, friend) reading this chapter together and studying the Scripture under "Expand Your Understanding" (*see* number one above).

6. *Sing the Truth*

> God has made me very special
> And I'm dearly loved by Him.
> Even though He knows me fully,
> He accepts me as I am.
> How I praise Him, how I praise Him,
> For His wondrous love for me,
> For His wondrous love for me.

(See page 15 for words and music for this song.)

2
You Are Deeply Loved

God has made you with a need to love and to be loved. For to love is really to live. To be loved is to experience the deepest kind of soul satisfaction. It is God's plan that you experience this *soul-satisfying* love through other people—family and friends. This is one way in which He wants to demonstrate to you something of what His love for you is like.

Just Because We Love You

"Both of my parents really made me feel loved," a Workshop woman wrote. "In many little ways they gave me the confidence that I was very special to them. Even after I lived away from home, my dad would ask me to drop by—just because 'we love you and want to see you.' I know I can call or visit my mother anytime and she will make me feel as though that call or visit just made her day."

Yet we human beings demonstrate this love so imperfectly that sometimes because of this, we find it difficult to believe that God really loves us. Or we fail to realize what real love is. So often people communicate to us that love or favor is conditional, based upon performance. Or it might even be that your idea of God's love, your parent's love, or another Christian's love, is that it is an obligation. One dear girl shared that even though her

parents provided her physical needs, she was sure they
didn't love her.

> I can remember trying to get them just to say, "I love
> you." They would scream, "Yes, I love you!" But that
> wasn't the way I wanted to hear it. Until last year I lived
> totally enveloped in a fantasy world—hooked on tran-
> quilizers, afraid to even go out of my house for fear of
> people, fear they would reject me.
> Even being married for seven years now, I couldn't
> believe even my husband loved me. Well, last October
> God did a 180-degree turn on me. I began to concentrate
> my attention on God's love for me as He reveals it in His
> Word. Where once I wouldn't even go to a missionary-
> circle meeting, now I can go and actually enjoy myself
> with others. I can go places with my new friends. I can
> accept myself and others. Because of God's love I have
> completely overcome my fantasy world. It no longer
> exists! And no more pills! Not one! I can't express how
> happy I have been these past five months. I am free! It's
> fantastic what God can do. I now have a clear mind and a
> clear heart, because God has proved to me through His
> Word that He loves me.

One supreme evidence of God's boundless love for
you is that while you were yet a sinner, God gave His
dearest treasure—Christ. When you were at your worst,
God gave His very best out of His unfathomable heart of
love for you (*see* Romans 5:8). Now that you are His
child, certainly He would not love you any less.

> He that spared not his own Son, but delivered him up
> for us all, how shall he not with him also freely give us all
> things?
>
>   Romans 8:32

Many times you may feel you are loved by people when you perform acceptably or impressively, but if you don't perform acceptably or impressively, then you aren't loved as much. God's love is not based upon performance. The song "Jesus loves me when I'm good, when I do the things I should; Jesus loves me when I'm bad, but it makes Him, oh, so sad," is true for child and adult alike. You may think that God's love changes, but it does not. Even when you are bad, selfish, or rebellious, He loves you just the same—unconditionally. No condition of your heart or mind or circumstances changes His love for you (*see* Romans 8:35–39). God loves you just as He loves His Son (*see* John 17:23), with a love that will never end. ". . . Yea, I have loved thee with an everlasting love: therefore with loving-kindness have I drawn thee" (Jeremiah 31:3).

Bask in God's Love

In order for you to have your own need for love met, you will need to bask long and often in God's love for you. One of the Workshop ladies shared that she grew up feeling unloved by her mother and having a dad who was usually too busy to spend much time with her. She went on to say:

This had a tremendous effect on me, to the point where I felt I would be better off in Heaven. My life verse was "For me to live is Christ, and to die is gain," with emphasis on the latter part! All of this has also had its effect on my husband and two children. After the Workshop last year I really sought the Lord and prayed and meditated on the verses you gave on the love of God until I really knew God does love me—the way I am right now. This was the first time I really knew and experienced His love so fully,

even though I had been a Christian many years. This has
been the beginning of the Lord working in my whole
family—things I had hoped for but didn't know how to
accomplish God has done in His own gracious way.

It is certainly true, we get some pictures and demon-
strations of God's love for us through our parents and
other people. However, you should not conclude that if
you had no father, or if your father was not good, wise,
loving, understanding, caring, that you cannot know or
sense that God is good, wise, loving, understanding, caring. J. I. Packer in *Knowing God* puts it this way.

> I have heard it seriously argued that the thought of di-
> vine fatherhood can mean nothing to those whose human
> father was inadequate, lacking wisdom, affection, or both,
> nor to those many more whose misfortune it was to have a
> fatherless upbringing . . . . it is just not true to suggest
> that in the realm of personal relations positive concepts
> cannot be formed by contrast . . . . the thought of our
> Maker becoming our perfect parent—faithful in love and
> care, generous and thoughtful, interested in all we do,
> respecting our individuality, skilful in training us, wise in
> guidance, always available, helping us to find ourselves in
> maturity, integrity, and uprightness—is a thought which
> can have meaning for everybody, whether we come to it
> by saying, "I had a wonderful father, and I see that God is
> like that, only more so," or by saying, "My father disap-
> pointed me here, and here, and here, but God, praise His
> name, will be very different," or even by saying, "I have
> never known what it is to have a father on earth, but thank
> God I now have one in heaven." [1]

To help in understanding God's love for you, think of
some things people have said or done which resulted in

your feeling they did not love you. Then remind yourself, "God isn't like that. He is very different in His
feeling toward me, in His actions toward me. He is a
Friend whose love is unfailing, everlasting, unwavering." Make a list of ways people have communicated
love to you. In response say, "I understand God is like
that, only much more so."

God has given us our Lord Jesus, not only as our Redeemer, but as a perfect human revelation of what God
is like. As we focus on Jesus' love—unwavering, unconditional, unmerited, everlasting, we see a human dem-
onstration of God's great love for us.

Glad to Be Me

Knowing the love that God has for us should help us to
have a proper and real love for ourselves, a "genuine and
joyful" acceptance of ourselves. You should be able to
say, "I'm glad to be me." This isn't pride or selfishness,
it's just agreeing with God that this part of His creation,
too, is very good. "And God saw every thing that He had
made, and, behold, it was very good . . ." (Genesis
1:31).

To have a proper love for self is the ability to feel good
about yourself. You can recognize and accept your
weaknesses and inabilities and deal with your sin. It is
to feel comfortable about yourself, to be at peace with
yourself, to feel *okay*, acceptable. It is not envying
another person's gifts, abilities, temperament. It is to be
content to be you, the person you are now for now, but
always having the aspiration to become more and more
the person God created you to be—more and more like
Jesus Christ. It is to have a godly desire to be continually
growing as a person, but in the process, knowing that

you are now a person of worth, of value, acceptable, lovable.

In addition, we must not only know, understand, and recognize through past experiences, the fact that God loves us; but in the midst of varied and sometimes mysterious events that God allows to touch us, we must believe God's love now. This is the walk of faith. In the midst of the hard-to-understand circumstances we must continue to believe in the love which has been so faithful in the past. In the midst of distressing situations such as a sudden death of a loved one, a wayward child, broken engagement, an accident, a failure in an assignment, loss of goods, God's love remains ever the same.

"We have known and believed the love that God hath to us" (1 John 4:16). Standing on the sure foundation of what we have proved God to be in the past, we may look on the present and future with perfect faith. We have known Him too well to doubt Him now. We have known, and now we believe. He has made no mistakes. He is making none. He has done the best, and is doing it. We do not understand His dealings, but we know Him who is behind the mystery of Providence, and can hear Him saying: "It is all right, only trust Me. Fear Not! It is I." [2]

O Blessed Heavenly Father, thank You for Your infinite, limitless, unconditional love for me. Thank You that You love me with an everlasting love which is not dependent upon circumstances or performance. Thank You that You love me when I'm my worst self as much as when I'm my best self. Your love is consistent and unchanging. I praise You! I realize my great need is to know and believe that You love me even when my own heart or circumstances seem to say the opposite. I pur-

*pose afresh to trust Your unfailing love which is more
tender and caring than any earthly mother or father's
love. Oh, how I praise You and love You. In Jesus' name,*
amen.

Turning Insight Into Action

1. Expand Your Understanding

After studying the following verses, write in your own
words how God conveys His deep and unchanging love
for you.

Jeremiah 31:3   Romans 8:31–39
Deuteronomy 7:7, 8   Ephesians 3:17–19
Romans 5:6–11

2. Search and Share

A college girl shared:

A girl on the next floor of our dorm often calls up the
steps to my roommate to ask her to come for an impromptu
party. Even though she knows I'm there, too, somehow
she always communicates by the tone of her voice that
I'm not wanted. It always hurts and makes me feel so
unloved.

Think of some particular circumstance or actions of
people which caused you to feel unloved. What were
your feelings and thoughts? What can you learn from this
hurtful situation that will be helpful as you communicate love to others?

3. Develop Your Awareness

During the coming week observe and write down at
least one way in which God has recently shown His love
to you through circumstances or people. It might be
something like this:

GOD HAS SAID

"Yea, I have loved thee
with an everlasting love"
(Jeremiah 31:3).

THEREFORE I MAY BOLDLY SAY

*I am
deeply
loved.*

We recently moved into an apartment complex. I have had a longing for Christian friends here. Last night when I went to get the mail, there was a notice hanging on the wall inviting anyone interested to join a Bible-study group. I'm really excited about it! God does care about the things we do and the friends we have. I'm thankful He has provided this fellowship for me. It's just one more indication of His love for me.

Make a list of present circumstances or situations in which you can now "know and believe the love God has for you." By faith know that God's love is working for you that which is best.

4. Store Up God's Thoughts

The Lord hath appeared of old unto me, saying, Yea, I have loved thee with an everlasting love: therefore with loving-kindness have I drawn thee.

Jeremiah 31:3

Store up God's thoughts by memorizing Jeremiah 31:3. Check other versions and paraphrases for expanded meaning. Read commentaries or handbooks on the Bible that are available to you. Let this verse become a part of your life.

5. Reach Out in Love

This week demonstrate your love to someone through some concrete actions. Choose one of the following ideas or let your imagination help you plan something special for someone.

(a) Study the Book of 1 John together with someone, particularly noting all references to God's love for you.

(b) Make cookies to share with a neighbor. Arrange an attractive plate, putting a small bow or flower at the side

for decoration. Try to sense how she would like them
presented. Would she enjoy a visit from you, so you
could both sit down for coffee and cookies? Or would
she enjoy cookies left at the door with a little note? Is
she too busy for a visit? Is she lonely and would enjoy a
visit?

(c) Surprise a member of your family by offering to
help with one of his regular tasks. Offer to do dishes for
your daughter, if that is her regular job. Offer to let Mom
have a morning off and get breakfast for the family, help
wax the car, or change a flat tire.

(d) Try to be sensitive to what would make someone
feel at home, loved, and special today. It might be simply listening to him. It might be laughing with him, as
one shared:

> I love to tease and play. If someone jokes back, I feel
> loved and wanted. Today in theology class I made a re-
> mark that was meant to be humorous. The teacher and the
> class laughed. This made me feel at home, accepted, of
> worth.

(e) Write a note or a letter to a missionary. Share a
verse or thought from the Bible that has been especially
meaningful to you recently. Think of some areas on
which to commend him. Use colorful, cheerful station-
ery.

(f) Help a busy or sick mother with housework, laun-
dry, or cooking for the family. Ask her for suggestions as
to what would be the most helpful to her.

6. Sing the Truth

> God has made me very special,
> And I'm dearly loved by Him.

Even though He knows me fully,
He accepts me as I am.
How I praise Him, how I praise Him,
For His wondrous love for me,
For His wondrous love for me.

(See page 15 for words and music for this song.)

3

You Are Fully Known, yet Fully Accepted

I have a friend who really accepts me for what I am. She knows more about me than anyone—my faults, my weaknesses, my insecurities—yet she doesn't make me feel inferior, unimportant. I feel like I'm a real person when I'm around her. She gives me the freedom to be me. I don't feel that I have to "put on" for her. I can cry or laugh, be quiet or talkative, share or withhold sharing. Even when there is a misunderstanding, I can report my feelings to her without her being threatened or hurt. We can share even our negative feelings and thoughts. She understands and identifies with me. She accepts me when my worst self shows as well as when my best self is forward. Well, she just accepts me as I am!

It's so comforting to have friends who love and accept you at all times—in varying moods and situations. Do you know that God is like that, only much more so?

God knows you through and through, yet He accepts you fully, totally, unconditionally. He knows all about you—your weaknesses, your insecurities, your failings, your fears, your inadequacies. Yet He says you are ". . . accepted in the beloved" (Ephesians 1:6). I like to say it this way, "accepted in the beloved"—period! No strings attached, no conditions to meet. "Wherefore receive ye one another, as Christ also received us to the glory of

God" (Romans 15:7). "Wherefore, accept one another, just as Christ also accepted us to the glory of God" (Romans 15:7 NAS).

God Accepts Me, if . . . .

Do you believe that God accepts you like that? I find that many well-meaning Christians have mental reservations about God's acceptance of them. In their thoughts, they say, "Yes, I know God accepts me, if I don't do . . . or if I do do . . . or when I become . . . ."

Some of these ideas have come from the way others have treated us. Such as:

My mother constantly criticized me while I was growing up. I could never do anything well enough for her.

I was a timid, shy person and was always most comfortable when hidden in a group. One evening as a group of young people were separating after a gathering, everyone was saying a general good-bye. But Miriam turned to me and said, "Good-bye, Evelyn, see you Sunday!" Words can't express the thrill that went through me—an actual physical reaction of warmth and a quickened heartbeat. I was a *person,* not just part of a crowd. And in those simple words she had communicated to me that I was accepted.

As a child and a teenager my dad often ignored me. In high school I was to go on a school trip and needed money. Dad ignored my need until I was ready to go out the door. Then he made me feel like a dog under the table waiting for some scraps. I was sure he hadn't accepted me as a daughter or even as a person.

One lady said, "Verna, I know God will accept me if I lose some weight." I said, "You must realize that God accepts you as you are now—fat." (I used that word just to emphasize His *unconditional* acceptance.) "Now true, it would be good for you to think of trimming down, but you must know that God accepts you as you are now and you must accept yourself as you are now."

Pretty, Like Karen

Sometimes you may feel that you're acceptable and accepted only when you are strong, or athletic, or successful, or pretty to look at. Lois wrote:

> When I was twelve years old, I brought a good friend home to play. When Daddy came home I introduced him to Karen. As soon as she went home he asked, "What was her name again?"
> "Karen. She's in my class at school."
> "Boy, she sure is a doll. I'll call her—the doll—instead of Karen."
> I remember thinking, "I wish Daddy thought I was a doll."

Unwittingly, Lois' father had communicated, "I don't accept you. You're not pretty like Karen."

Or it might be you feel that God or others accept you as they think you are, but they do not really know you. You may reason that if they really knew you, they wouldn't accept you. God knows you fully, totally.

> O Lord, thou hast searched me, and known me. Thou knowest my downsitting and mine uprising, thou understandest my thought afar off. Thou compassest my path and my lying down, and art acquainted with all my ways. For there is not a word in my tongue, but, lo, O Lord, thou knowest it altogether.
>
> Psalms 139:1–4

GOD HAS SAID

"O Lord, Thou hast searched me,
and known me" (Psalms 139:1).
"He hath made us accepted
in the beloved" (Ephesians 1:6).

THEREFORE I MAY BOLDLY SAY

*I am
fully known,
yet fully accepted.*

He knows you totally—yet totally accepts you. He is continually aware of and knows all about you, as the above Scripture says. He knows when you sit down, when you rise up, what your thoughts are even before you think them. He knows where you walk and what you do and what you are like, yet He deeply loves and totally accepts you. He accepts you without reservation.

He accepts you with the gifts and abilities He has given you. He wants you to be very careful to develop these and employ them for service to Him and to other people. You may feel unacceptable to others because of your "lack" of gifts and abilities as you view it. Or if you have many gifts and abilities, you may sense that some people are jealous of you and withhold acceptance of you. If either of these is your position, know that God accepts you fully.

Forgiveness and Acceptance

He accepts you in spite of your sins. Of course, when we sin we need to immediately come to Him, confess that sin, receive His forgiveness, and enter afresh into the awareness of His full acceptance.

He does not withdraw His acceptance because you have sinned. His acceptance, as His love, is not conditioned on our performance. Though, of course, to enjoy the awareness of His acceptance and love, we need to be continually cleansed from all unrighteousness.

But if we walk in the light, as he is in the light, we have fellowship one with another, and the blood of Jesus Christ his Son cleanseth us from all sin . . . . If we confess our sins, he is faithful and just to forgive us our sins, and to cleanse us from all unrighteousness.

1 John 1:7, 9

A single girl said, "Verna, I know that I will never make a worthy wife." She went on to share how she had gotten involved sexually. Though she had confessed her sin, she felt she was not now totally acceptable. She even thought she should look for and marry an "unworthy" husband, because she would never make a "worthy" wife. God's forgiving grace and His "accepting us in the beloved" is for this very need. He grants it to us when we don't deserve it. He accepts us when we deserve the very opposite.

To say that God knows me fully is saying that He knows the worst that is in me. He will never be shocked at anything I might think or do. He sees more pride, selfishness, stubbornness in me than I even see in myself. Yet He loves me, has redeemed me, accepted me. He has adopted me into His family as His own dearly loved child and promises to continually watch over me for good.

Oh, glorious truth—fully known, yet fully accepted!

Loving, forgiving Father, how I praise You for Your mercy and Your unfailing love. Thank You for accepting me fully, even though You know all about my failings, my weaknesses, my sins, my conflicts and frustrations. Thank You that I am accepted in the Beloved. How I praise You! In Jesus' name, amen.

Turning Insight Into Action

1. Expand Your Understanding

From the following verses make a list of ways which indicate God knows you fully and write one statement which indicates He accepts you as you are.

Psalms 139:1–6
Ephesians 1:3–14

2. Search and Share

Think of a time when you were aware another knew you did something wrong but still accepted you. Share how that acceptance motivated you to change. Or think of a time when you felt unaccepted because of your seeming lack of gifts or abilities. Share how you felt and how it caused you to change your course of action. Notice the conclusion this girl came to:

As far back as I can remember, my father never praised or commended anything I ever did. The more I tried to please him, the more he tore me down. I was always the "stupidest," "ugliest," and worst person around. My parents both worked, and I was left with responsibility for the housework when I was very young. I always made supper, but no matter what I made, it wasn't cooked right. My father still feels this way about me now, even though I'm married. In his eyes I married the wrong man, had girls instead of boys, and am serving Christ instead of the world. In my father's eyes I'm a failure, but in my Father's eyes I'm somebody. Praise the Lord!

3. Develop Your Awareness

Write three answers to the statement, "I feel most loved when . . . ."

From John 4:1–26 and/or John 8:1–11, summarize how Jesus demonstrated knowledge of and yet full acceptance of the person. This week observe occasions when people have demonstrated the same accepting attitude toward you. Jot down an illustration.

4. Store Up God's Thoughts

"O Lord, thou hast searched me, and known me" (Psalms 139:1).

"To the praise of the glory of his grace, wherein he hath made us accepted in the beloved" (Ephesians 1:6).

5. Reach Out in Love

This week demonstrate your acceptance of someone. Choose one of the following or create your own project for your own particular situation.

(a) Take a treat to or do a deed of kindness for someone against whom you have entertained hard, negative thoughts.

(b) Ask another for his choice of a game to play or a book to read together.

(c) When someone comes to you at a very busy time, demonstrate that you have time for them instead of being *too busy*.

"I attend a rather large Bible-study group," one shared. "As I was leaving last week I asked one of the leaders if she had a minute to talk to me. She was busy at the time answering the questions of the women as they left, but she said, 'Certainly,' and immediately sat down beside me and gave her full attention to me.

"After quite a lengthy discussion, we parted. The following Monday she called and invited me to lunch at her home because she said she didn't feel we had finished. She was not *too busy* to give me her time and her genuine concern."

(d) If you are in a position of authority over anyone—supervisor, teacher, parent, baby-sitter, and so forth, plan how to speak words of appreciation for what those under you are doing *right*. Glenda's experience as a dorm mother in a boarding school shows how important it is to notice what others do right.

Upon my arrival my responsibilities were clearly laid out for me by the dorm coordinator. I really appreciated this, because I had never held such a position before. Time went on and I was taking more and more of the responsibility. But the coordinator told me only the things I was doing wrong or what I needed to do. I never heard of anything I was doing right, so I felt I was doing nothing right and was really of no worth to my girls, or to the school.

(e) Together with someone, go through the Book of Mark and list all the occasions when Jesus showed concern for and gave His time to individuals.

6. *Sing the Truth*

> God has made me very special,
> And I'm dearly loved by Him.
> Even though He knows me fully,
> He accepts me as I am.
> How I praise Him, how I praise Him,
> For His wondrous love for me,
> For His wondrous love for me.

4

You Are a Person in Process

As God's redeemed child, His loving goal for me is to become more and more like Jesus Christ. What an honor and precious privilege to demonstrate by my attitudes, words, and actions what He is really like! "As thou hast sent me into the world, even so have I also sent them into the world" (John 17:18). "For whom he did foreknow, he also did predestinate to be conformed to the image of his Son . . ." (Romans 8:29).

It's helpful for me to realize I'm a person in process—not yet fully like Him but becoming more and more like Him as I daily yield to Him and cooperate with Him. This "being conformed to the image of Jesus Christ" is a lifelong process.

It is good to know that I'm His workmanship. It is He that is working. I'm under His loving, caring supervision, and He is doing the work. We are the clay and He is the Potter. Our responsibility is to cooperate with Him, yield to Him, trust Him; He is to do the work. "For we are his workmanship, created in Christ Jesus unto good works . . ." (Ephesians 2:10). And, oh, it is good to know that He considers me so precious to Him that He undertakes to complete His work successfully. He promises to continue His faithful work until my life on this earth ends.

Being confident of this very thing, that he which hath
begun a good work in you will perform it until the day of
Jesus Christ.

Philippians 1:6

He undertakes to accomplish this even though He
knows some of the difficulties I will cause Him because
of my selfishness, willfulness, stubbornness. He knows I
need to be purified—refined as gold needs to be refined.
In the process, I need to be renewed in my mind, emo-
tions, and will, to be delivered from following my own
natural inclinations, and to learn to listen to and obey the
promptings of the Holy Spirit.

Cooperation of Confident Trust

One way He will build in me these Christlike qualities is, in His loving wisdom, to allow difficulties, trials,
failures, misunderstandings by others, problems. My response in the midst of these situations will be the key in
building this godly character, becoming more and more
like Jesus Christ. This is where my cooperation of
confident trust is needed.

Paul shares with us in Romans 5:3–5 that our response
is the essential thing. We are to "glory in tribulations."
G-l-o-r-y doesn't spell *growl!* If we glory in them, take
them in the right spirit, have the right response to them,
these things will be used by God to develop the godly
qualities in us. James says the same thing in these
words: "Consider it all joy, my brethren, when you encounter various trials, knowing that the testing of your
faith produces endurance" (James 1:2, 3 NAS). God will
use it to your benefit as it builds into a character of patience, steadfastness, and endurance. God's free and effective work in our lives depends on our response of

trust and confidence. It is so essential that we trust Him rather than having an attitude of resentment or complaining or blaming others (or God) for our difficulties.

We should learn to view our difficulties and trials as opportunities "to make a highway for our God." Therefore, we are to glory in tribulations, to count it all joy when difficulties and trials come to us, knowing God has allowed this to touch us in this way and He will work it together for good (*see* Romans 8:28). God faithfully disciplines (or trains) His children that He might bring forth the peaceable fruit of righteousness in those who have the correct response—those who are "exercised thereby" (*see* Hebrews 12:11).

One of the most common trials we are faced with is a health problem, a physical need. A Workshop lady shares how she learned to trust through a time of sickness:

My second trip back to the hospital for a breast tumor was a fearful thing. The first trip (during which the tumor was found to be malignant) I had trusted God to see me through, and He did. But this trip . . . I knew now what it could and would mean—real suffering, plus the knowledge that this might be "the beginning of the end." I thought of my two small children.

When panic was getting really bad, I remembered to thank God and trust Him. I got out my Bible. It contained promises for me. Are they true or not? I sat down and started thanking God for each promise, saying to myself, "Is this true for me?" "Casting all your care upon him, for he careth for you" (1 Peter 5:7). What a promise! I just thanked Him for caring for me. If He really cared for me, I wouldn't go through anything that wasn't really necessary. If He cared for me, He also took the concern for my little ones. I made a definite decision to thank Him for His love, care, and concern for me. After this, whenever the panic started to rise, I just had to thank Him for caring for me, and for being such a great God!

The second and third trips to the hospital did not reveal any malignancy. But I can truly say I grew tremendously as a trusting Christian through these trying times. Now, two years away from this, I continue to thank Him for sending me through these things that have helped me to depend on my caring God.

One simple, significant way of verbalizing our cooperation and confident trust is to say, "Thank You," recognize He's in control, and for some reason He has allowed this to touch us and will cause it to result in *our* good as well as *His* good.

Growing in Relationships

Another aspect of this lifelong process of maturing is our growing in relationships—oneness with God, oneness with other persons.

> Neither pray I for these alone, but for them also which shall believe on me through their word; That they all may be one; as thou, Father, art in me, and I in thee, that they also may be one in us: that the world may believe that thou hast sent me.
>
> John 17:20, 21

God's goal for me as a person in process is full maturity, fully integrating my life into His life, His will, His viewpoint, His desires. In the process of becoming this person, I develop a growing love relationship with the Lord. I learn to increasingly draw upon Him and His power and adequacy for all my needs. Our oneness deepens. His will becomes my will; His viewpoint, mine. I venture to let God love me, and I find He can be utterly trusted. He does love. He does care. He is good!

God has made us with a need to relate to other people as well. Indeed, He has even prayed that we might know the same oneness of soul that He shared with the Father. Developing a meaningful relationship with others is essential if we are to continue to be persons in process. We need the comfort of the love of others, therefore we also need to deliberately and trustfully go out in love to others and to share our real selves with others. Our gifts, abilities, achievements alone will not comfort us.

No one can really love you deeply unless he begins to understand you. And he cannot understand you unless you share who you are. Through sharing yourself with others you can be loved and understood by them. Many are afraid to reveal who they really are—they are afraid of not being understood, afraid of not being able to express how they really do feel, afraid the other person may not understand the tremendous importance of this sharing or afraid he may not keep their confidence, afraid he may use it against them, judge them, condemn or ridicule them, or be angry with them. Maybe you have taken this risk before and have been disappointed and have thus withdrawn all the more from open sharing. You are doubly fearful. But you must take the risk again or you will experience real inner isolation and loneliness.

Prayerfully consider with whom you might share. Choose one whom you could trust, and take the risk, trusting the Lord for the outcome. When you allow yourself to be known, you will find people to be more understanding, more loving, more affirming, more reassuring,

GOD HAS SAID

"Being confident of this very thing,
that he which hath begun a good work
in you will perform it until the day
of Jesus Christ" (Philippians 1:6).

THEREFORE I MAY BOLDLY SAY

I am
a person
in process.

more considerate than you ever dreamed possible. This will be a very freeing, growing experience as you find you have been listened to, taken seriously, and understood. The other is confirming his love to you and affirming your worth as a person, and you experience another step in the growth process—a friendship has been deepened, and you have both grown as persons.

Take the Risk—Become Involved

To grow in a deeply satisfying relationship with another person, you need to commit yourself to him by identifying with his interests, concerns, joys, sorrows. Persons grow as friendship between them grows. Friendship grows as you open your hearts to each other, sharing each other's concerns, thoughts, feelings. Take the risk that is feared and grow as a person. This same principle applies in your growing friendship with the Lord. There will need to be a personal commitment to Him. Open your heart to receive His love, trust His unfailing kindness. Commit yourself to His interests, His concerns. Take the risk of relinquishing your self-interests and self-concerns. Become involved with Him in His great purposes for you in His vast, world cause. You will experience continual personal enlargement—growth.

"I'm not all that I should be. I'm not yet what I shall be. But I'm thankful I'm not what I used to be." I'm growing! Many times alumnae in the Enriched Living Workshops say:

> Verna, it's so good to be back again! This time I can see so many principles I've been applying, and I didn't even realize it. It's been so good to review the sessions again, because I can see progress that I was unaware of.

Then she will go on to share thrilling evidences of growth as a person and in her relationships.

Each of us is a person in the process of becoming. We have grown, but there is continual need for more growth as a person. Ultimately I'm to become a fully mature, perfect, complete person—one like Jesus Christ.

Beloved, now are we the sons of God, and it doth not yet appear what we shall be: but we know that, when he shall appear, we shall be like him; for we shall see him as he is.

1 John 3:2

O loving Heavenly Father, how assuring to know that You are tenderly watching over Your work in and through me. You work with precision, accuracy, and love. How I praise You for Your loving, faithful work. Thank You that You have not left me to myself to develop and become the best I can, but You have undertaken to make me a person who demonstrates the qualities of Jesus Christ as I cooperate with You. I thank You that You will continue to help me grow as a person and in my relationships with You and with others. Thank You for Your patience and love as I am in the process of becoming more and more like Jesus. In His name, amen.

Turning Insight Into Action

1. *Expand Your Understanding*

From Romans 8:29; 2 Corinthians 4:10, 11; Matthew 5:13–16 jot down concisely what God's goal for you is.

From the truths in Ephesians 2:10; Philippians 1:6, 2:13; Psalms 138:8 formulate a statement that indicates how God will accomplish His goal for you.

2. Search and Share
Describe something of the difficult situation of one or more of these Bible characters. What were their responses in the situation? What character quality was shown?

Paul, 2 Corinthians 4–6
Paul and Silas, Acts 16
Joseph, Genesis 37, 39–45
David and his brothers, 1 Samuel 17
David and Saul, 1 Samuel 24, 26
Peter, Luke 22:31–34; Luke 22:54–62; Acts 2:14–47

Share a time when you were in a very difficult situation—misunderstood by others, mistreated by others, falsely accused, or pressed by an intense trial. What was your response? How did the Lord strengthen and comfort you?

3. Develop Your Awareness
Ask at least three people how a trial, suffering, or loss brought them into a more trusting, loving relationship with their Heavenly Father. If they are able to remember, have them share the Scripture God used to encourage and strengthen them.

Make a list of specific character qualities you would like to see developed in your life. Ask God each morning to work these in you that day.

4. Store Up God's Thoughts
"Being confident of this very thing, that he which hath begun a good work in you will perform it until the day of Jesus Christ" (Philippians 1:6).

Additional verse for memory—Ephesians 2:10.

5. Reach Out in Love
Think of ways you might help someone else in the midst of a trying situation.

(a) Take dinner to a family where there is a sickness or a special need.

(b) Phone someone who lives alone for a brief, cheery visit.

(c) Be sensitive to someone who is discouraged over a failure or hurt by another's words or actions. Speak a few words of comfort or encouragement to them. Share verses of Scripture that have helped you, or send them a brief, kind note.

(d) Remember that the routine activities sometimes become a trying situation. Take special notice today of the regular, expected duties others around you faithfully perform (washing dishes, mowing the lawn, straightening up the house, repairing things). Express appreciation to them specifically for these things.

(e) Actively take part in someone else's life and interests this week. Listen to, look at, or enjoy their hobby—piano, garden, craft. Attend a game or other school function that your child is involved in.

(f) With a friend memorize James 1:2–8 as an encouragement to each other to respond to trials in the godly way.

(g) Be aware if someone has a special need for help in an area in which you have ability or skills. Offer your assistance. One father shared how a friend saw his need, helped him through a difficult situation, and opened up a whole new world of interest to him.

Just before Christmas our son's Volkswagen engine "blew up." He needed it daily to go to school, but we just couldn't afford to get it repaired. A Christian friend who is a mechanic freely offered to help overhaul the engine. Having no VW experience, I would never have tackled it by myself, but with his kind offer I confidently agreed to help. We worked together, slowly and carefully. When completed, it ran beautifully—and for many thousands of miles since. We were successful! A few months later our daughter's VW engine "blew up." You guessed it. I tackled it alone and was successful. I was amazed that I was fascinated by doing VW engine overhauls. What was once a dreaded fear has now become a useful hobby—buying tired old VW's, repairing them, and selling them to help our son through college.

6. Sing the Truth

> I am still a person in process,
> Workmanship of God's own hand.
> Even though so deeply fallen,
> I'm redeemed by His great grace.
> How I praise Him, how I praise Him,
> For His wondrous grace to me,
> For His wondrous grace to me.

5

You Are God's Redeemed Child

We human beings have the unique privilege of being created in the image of God. We have a mind to think, to will. We have the power to choose, to understand, to love. What a privilege to be made in His likeness. None other of God's created earth creatures have this unique and wonderful privilege.

> Then God said, "Let Us make man in Our image, according to Our likeness . . . ." And God created man in His own image, in the image of God He created him . . . .
>
> Genesis 1:26, 27 NAS

However, man has deeply fallen from this position, and the image of God in him is badly marred. Through Adam's sin we inherited our sinful nature.

> Wherefore, as by one man sin entered into the world, and death by sin; and so death passed upon all men, for that all have sinned.
>
> Romans 5:12

Because of this and because of our own personal sin—determination to go our own way—we became alienated from the life of God. We are sinners by nature and by personal choice. As a result, our fellowship with

God was cut off and His design for us to reflect His image and bring glory to His name was short-circuited.

God Gave His Dearest Treasure

Being deeply fallen does not mean that we are non-persons or that, as His creation, we are of no value. No, the *person* is of value but "The *heart* is deceitful above all things, and desperately wicked . . ." (Jeremiah 17:9, italics mine). That is, the heart is no good because of sin and the sinful nature, but that does not mean that the person is no good. Personal worth and human dignity remain. In fact, we are of such value to Him, so precious to Him, that God gave up His dearest treasure, His only begotten and much-loved Son to die for us. Jesus very willingly left the glories of Heaven to live on this earth for a time and then to go to the cross to die in our behalf for our sins.

This earth was not always pleasant for Him—*nothing* compared to the glories and comforts of Heaven, where He was surrounded by praise and honor. Here He was mocked, ridiculed, misunderstood, mistreated, spit upon, beaten, and finally nailed to the cross. Even before He came He knew all this would happen to Him, yet He considered us persons of value, of worth. He loved us and wanted to redeem us so that we might be restored to a place of fellowship with Him, to love Him and enjoy Him. He knew that only in this way could we realize our true worth and be happy and fulfilled and bring glory to His name, as we were created to do. "But God commendeth His love toward us, in that, while we were yet sinners, Christ died for us" (Romans 5:8).

As we recognize that to Him we have always been persons of worth, we do not wish in any way to diminish how deeply we are fallen. The Bible clearly

describes the depth of human sin—your sin and mine.
"But we are all as an unclean thing, and all our righ-
teousnesses are as filthy rags . . ." (Isaiah 64:6). "For all
have sinned, and come short of the glory of God" (Romans 3:23).

"If we say that we have no sin, we deceive ourselves,
and the truth is not in us" (1 John 1:8). We see it in our
own heart; we see it in the world about us. Sin is simply
going our own way, independent of God's way (*see*
Isaiah 53:6). We have all fallen short of perfectly living
up to God's standard of righteousness, of holiness. We
have sinned, and the sin principle of selfishness and
independence of God—going our own way instead of
His—is deeply ingrained in our nature. It is the inclina-
tion of the flesh.

The tremendous price Jesus Christ was willing to pay
to redeem us from our sins gives us some clue as to the
value He places upon us. It was Jesus' very lifeblood.
We are ". . . not redeemed with corruptible things, as
silver and gold . . . But with the precious blood of
Christ . . ." (1 Peter 1:18, 19). Nothing less could answer the need or pay the price. What a price! What persons of value and worth we are to Him! For a person to
become God's redeemed child he needs to make a definite, deliberate commitment of himself to God and receive Jesus Christ to be his Saviour and Lord. If you
have never made this commitment, I would encourage
you to pause right now. Pray to Him, acknowledging
your sin. Thank Him that Jesus died to pay the penalty of
your sin. Ask Him to enter your life and become your
Saviour and Lord and thank Him that now you are His
child. Upon such a simple invitation Jesus Christ will
enter your life, forgive your sin, and make you His redeemed child (*see* John 1:12; Revelation 3:20; John
3:36).

A teenager wrote down for me what this marvel of redemption means to her:

> The fact that God loves me enough to have sent Jesus to save me is overwhelming. And then God really forgives me for my sin! What's really neat is that He's working with me and He's willing to wait for me as I grow, and even as I fail. He has a potential for me—He's got it all worked out. I think what amazes me a lot right now is that God forgives me over and over totally!

Of Worth, but Not Worthy

Though we always have been and are of immense worth to God, this does not in any way imply we are *worthy*. We have not earned, nor do we deserve, the privilege of any of His benefits or blessings. No, we never did anything to deserve His grace, mercy, or redemption, nor shall we ever deserve it or earn it. But He freely bestows upon us His mercy and grace out of His great storehouse of love for us, even though we really deserve exactly the opposite because of our sin.

Through faith in Jesus Christ we can be God's redeemed children! Through His blood our sins are forgiven and we have the privilege of fellowship with Him. He has adopted us into His family. *We are children of the Heavenly Father*—with all the privileges and benefits of beloved children! In addition to all of this, redemption involves power over the sin principle and life with Him in the future. Our challenge then is to live as honorable children of the Heavenly Father should live. For this need He has not left us to ourselves. He not only redeems me, but God Himself comes to live within me. My body becomes the temple of the Holy Spirit.

What? know ye not that your body is the temple of the Holy Ghost which is in you, which ye have of God, and ye are not your own?

1 Corinthians 6:19

His life is a life of power. Now I have tremendous capabilities that otherwise would not be mine. The Almighty One lives in me! "I can do all things through Christ which strengtheneth me" (Philippians 4:13).

I not only have the Holy Spirit resident within, I also have the promises of God to appropriate by faith.

There hath no temptation taken you but such as is common to man: but God is faithful, who will not suffer you to be tempted above that ye are able . . . .

1 Corinthians 10:13

Let us therefore come boldly unto the throne of grace, that we may obtain mercy, and find grace to help in time of need.

Hebrews 4:16

. . . My grace is sufficient for thee . . . .

2 Corinthians 12:9

There will be times when I will fail to appropriate all that is mine in Christ. When this happens I need to come again to His throne of mercy, ask His forgiveness, accept it, then go forward again. He never gives up on me, or gets impatient with me, or tires of my coming. We can come and come again. He is always there and His patience and mercy "endure forever." How good is the God we adore!

GOD HAS SAID

"Ye were not redeemed
with corruptible things . . .
But with the precious blood
of Christ" (1 Peter 1:18, 19).

THEREFORE I MAY BOLDLY SAY

*I am
God's
redeemed child.*

Complete Redemption

His redemption not only provides freedom from the guilt of sin and freedom from the power of sin, but it also gives us freedom from the presence of sin. We may share life with Him in eternity!

> And if I go and prepare a place for you, I will come again, and receive you unto myself; that where I am, there ye may be also.
>
> John 14:3

Oh, what full, what complete redemption! What mercy, what grace, what love! Because of Jesus we now have ". . . redemption through his blood, even the forgiveness of sins" (Colossians 1:14).

Many times the enemy, "the accuser of the brethren," tries to keep the child of God feeling guilty over forgiven sin, that is, sin that has been brought to Jesus, confessed, and cleansed. A Workshop lady expressed it this way: "Verna, I can believe that God forgives me, but I cannot forgive myself." You will be able to forgive yourself only as you really believe in and fully accept the fact that God forgives you. Bask in His forgiveness. Memorize such Scriptures as Psalms 103:12; 1 John 1:9; Hebrews 8:12; Isaiah 44:22; Isaiah 1:18; 1 John 1:7; Colossians 1:14. It is very important to agree with God. Accept these words of His as true. Take the comfort of them. Thank God for forgiveness even if you don't feel forgiven. Sing verses of songs which speak of God's forgiveness. Let the glorious message of God's forgiveness give your heart peace and rest.

O loving Saviour, thank You for redeeming me, for paying the price for my sins, for forgiving all my sins.

*Thank You for helping me to be victorious over the
promptings of sin in my life. Help me ever to honor You
with my life and be an instrument of bringing glory to
You here on this earth. In Your loving, powerful name,*
amen.

Turning Insight Into Action

1. Expand Your Understanding
Read and study the following Scriptures:

> Jeremiah 17:9
> Romans 3:10–12, 20–24; 5:6–9
> Isaiah 53:1–9
> 1 John 1:7–10
> 1 Peter 1:18–20; 2:24, 25

From the Romans verses formulate a statement which
indicates God says each of us is deeply fallen, a sinner
by nature and practice. From 1 Peter 1:18–20 and 2:24
describe how our redemption has been accomplished.

2. Search and Share
What were some of the sufferings Jesus was willing to
endure to give you redemption? Refer to Isaiah 53 and
Mark 15. Share how the sufferings of Jesus on your behalf speak to you of your value, worth to Him.

3. Develop Your Awareness
During this week look for special benefits which are
yours because you are God's redeemed child, such as
freedom from guilt of sin, continual cleansing from sins,
and so forth. Make a list of these. You might refer to
Scripture mentioned in previous chapters also. This
could be the beginning of a notebook just between you
and God. One shared that her "Blessing Notebook"
grew to include many things.

I also write in my notebook the thoughts I have as I read God's Word each day. I note when He answers my prayers. Included in my blessings is a list of people who have told me they love me or have expressed their love in other ways. There are songs written in it, songs that have helped to center my mind on God. When I feel down, I refer to my notebook and to Scripture I have underlined in my Bible.

4. Store Up God's Thoughts

". . . ye were not redeemed with corruptible things . . . But with the precious blood of Christ . . ." (1 Peter 1:18, 19).

Additional verses for memory—1 Peter 2:24; 2 Corinthians 5:21.

5. Reach Out in Love

The basis of all our blessings, privileges, peace, service, and love for others is the redemption we have in Christ Jesus. Choose one or more of the following projects with which to share with others the wonder of your redemption.

(a) Share with someone the blessing of forgiveness of sin and your new life in Christ. It will strengthen you to verbalize your thankfulness and it will turn your friend's thoughts toward God and His offered redemption through Christ.

(b) When we are redeemed, we belong to that wonderful body called the "household of faith." Galatians 6:10 tells us to do good to all men, but especially to the "household of faith." Plan specifically what you can do this week for someone else in the Body of Christ. (Check "Turning Insight Into Action" in previous chapter, if you need help.)

(c) Another privilege we have as God's redeemed

children is to pray for each other (*see* James 5:16). This
week set aside a few extra minutes each day to pray for
the specific needs of one other person.

(d) Through a specific deed demonstrate love to
someone who has mistreated or misunderstood you.
Through this special deed you will demonstrate God's
forgiveness. You might offer to take her shopping for her
groceries or other needs, bake a special treat for the family, offer to baby-sit while she has a morning out, mow
his lawn, help repair his car, and so forth.

6. Sing the Truth

> I am still a person in process,
> Workmanship of God's own hand.
> Even though so deeply fallen,
> I'm redeemed by His great grace.
> How I praise Him, how I praise Him,
> For His wondrous grace to me,
> For His wondrous grace to me.

6
You Are a Person of Value

Our four-year-old, Jolene, sat nearby as I was studying for my weekly Bible class. As she struggled with the pictures she was making she kept saying, "Oh, I can never make anything good enough!" Screwing up her face in painful thought, she tried again, only to repeat, a bit more exasperated than before, "I can never make anything good enough!" When I sensed her inner struggle, I tried to encourage her and asked her why she felt that way. She continued intensely on the picture, but said quietly, "I can never make anything good enough—you always throw away everything I make." What a horrible realization that was! It was true, at the end of the day I would gather up her then forgotten scribblings and cuttings and throw them away. The message was getting through to her that nothing she ever made was "good enough." I asked her forgiveness and told her that I was sorry I had given her that impression. Then I took a paper sack and wrote her name on it and told her it was especially to keep her drawings. She was all smiles again.

Like Jolene, some of us have the idea that the "little drawings" of our daily lives are worthless, of no use, good only to be thrown out at the end of the day. God has other ideas. Think of the value that He has placed upon you. In God's estimate you are important enough for

Jesus Christ to step out of the glory world to come down
to earth and redeem you. What value! What worth!

Not only that, but He adopted you as His child and
makes you a member of His family. Now you are a son of
the living God and, with Jesus, a joint heir to all of the
riches of Heaven (*see* Romans 8:17). For a poor, help-
less, lonely child to be taken into a wealthy, loving, caring family would indeed be a privilege, an honor, a comfort, a security. But for you to be taken into God's family
as an adopted son is a much higher, nobler privilege and
honor. He affords much more comfort, security, honor,
than the wealthiest and best earthly parents could supply. You are even "blessed with all spiritual blessings in
Christ" (*see* Ephesians 1:3).

Glad We're Friends

That we are of value is obvious as we observe how He
further underscores the intimate relationship He desires
to have with us by calling us friends.

> Henceforth I call you not servants; for the servant
> knoweth not what his lord doeth: but I have called you
> friends; for all things that I have heard of my Father I
> have made known unto you.
>
> John 15:15

What are the qualities of the best earthly friend? One
in whom you can confide—your best thoughts, your
worst thoughts. One who is there in time of need, de-
pendable, trustworthy. One with whom you feel comfortable because you know he understands, loves, and
accepts you in all the varying moods of life.

When you're joyful, your friend wants to share your

joy. When you're sad and discouraged, your friend wants you to feel free to trust him with these feelings. Your friend wants the honor of supporting you, upholding you, doing something for you to help you in your distress, praying for you, encouraging you. When you are lonely, your friend wants to give you the support of his presence, his listening ear. Friends smile together, laugh together, cry together, play together, work together. Togetherness is the joy of friendship.

Why is the greeting-card market full of cards with simple words expressing a vote of friendship or love? Why do you appreciate receiving one of these cards from a friend? Even though the words may be so simple, it affirms your value as a person and confirms your friend's love to you. What comfort, what joy! Someone loves, appreciates, cares, and wants me for a friend. Simple words such as "Glad we're friends," or "To my very special friend," can brighten our whole day.

Jesus says, in effect, "I want you to know that it is My desire to have this relationship to you—I have called you friends." (*See* John 15:14, 15.)

All of us have been disappointed in friendships at one time or another. At best, our friends—the greatest and best—are imperfect. Jesus is not that kind of friend. He does not vary in His friendship toward us even if we vary. He is a faithful, unchangeable friend, the like of which we have not experienced in any earthly friendship.

We are afraid even our close friends might discover things about us that will cause them to like us less—not so with Jesus. Since He is all-knowing, He knows all about us—past and present. He knows our varying moods and degrees of future faithfulness. Knowing all this, He wants us to be His friends. He won't be surprised or shocked at anything we might think or do. He will never change His mind about our friendship.

As a friend, He wants to be to you what you need. He wants to give good things to you. He wants to enhance your joy, your sense of being loved. He wants you to have peace. He desires for you all that any good friend could desire—and much, much more—infinitely more.

When someone who is honorable, unselfish, and loving wants to be a friend to us, we feel so good. We feel of value, of worth, and are deeply encouraged. We tend to feel more comfortable about ourselves if they indicate they feel comfortable about us and put such value upon us. Just the slightest indication that they want to be our friend is noticed and deeply appreciated. Jesus is such a friend.

Be My Daddy Again

He is always there, ready to listen. Never distracted, never too weary or too busy, always ready to help in time of need. A little girl was beginning to feel the busyness of her daddy. Her mother tells the story:

> Our daughter was a few weeks from turning four. My husband was finishing Bible school with plans to go into the ministry. One day while talking to her he asked if she wanted him to become a pastor. She responded with, "No." He explained that he was to obey God the same as she was. Did she want him to obey God? "Yes." Well, God wanted Dad to be a pastor. She thought about this awhile, then said, "Dad, when you finish being a pastor, will you be my daddy again?"

God is never too busy to be our Father, our Friend. What greater way could He affirm our value and confirm His love to us than to say, "I want to be your Friend, and I want you to be My friend!" The eternal, living, powerful, omnipotent, faithful, unchangeable God, my Heavenly Father, is my personal Friend!

In Partnership

He also affirms my value to Him by calling me to work with Him. He takes me on His staff and gives me the privilege of being in partnership with Him in His world-saving ministries—redeeming, reconciling, enriching lives. This is how one new Christian began to realize the joy of this partnership:

> Two years ago the Lord used my husband and me to lead my nine-year-old sister to Himself. My husband and I had been saved six months. We had both been on drugs and we had exposed my little sister to them. When we accepted the Lord my little sister saw the wonderful change. That summer she came to our home for a week's vacation. This particular week happened to be Vacation Bible School at our church. We went, so she did, too. The Lord used the teacher to plant the question, used me to water it, and God reaped the increase. I really felt like someone of special value to God because He actually used me to lead another soul to Himself. And what a special privilege it was to me, because it was someone so dear to me—my own little sister.

In His Word in 2 Corinthians 5:18–20; 6:1, 4, He expresses this partnership in so many ways:

> We have been given the ministry of reconciliation.
> He has committed to us the word of reconciliation.
> We are ambassadors for Christ.

We are workers together with Him.
We are ministers of God.

"God is faithful, by whom ye were called unto the
fellowship of his Son Jesus Christ our Lord" (1 Corinthians 1:9). The word for fellowship here is the same as that
used of James and John being partners with Simon (*see*
Luke 5:10). We have been called into partnership with
the Son of God, as F. B. Meyer expresses it:

In His redemptive purposes, His love and tears for
men, and ultimately in His triumph and glory, Christ
often speaks of Himself as the "sent One"; but He graciously invites His disciples and friends, saying, "*We
must work.*" It is as though He said, "I have a designated
work which must be done; but I cannot do it alone. We
must do it—you and I, together." Every crop that goldens
in the summer wind is due to the summons of the God of
Nature to the husbandman, "Come and let us work together, thou and I." Every achievement in factory or mill
is due to the combination of the divine laws and the
human agency. We must work, is God's constant appeal.
We have been called into the fellowship or partnership of
the Son of God. He does not say, go, but come; not do this,
but let us do it. He has set His heart on the glory of the
Father, and He calls us to cooperate with Him in bringing
back men to God.[3]

*O holy Father, I can only bow before You in awesome
wonder that You have looked upon me; You've forgiven
me, adopted me as Your own child, called me Your
friend, and given me the privilege of being Your servant
in Your world enterprises. Oh, by Your Holy Spirit, help
me to be an honorable child, a good friend, and a faith-*

GOD HAS SAID

"Behold, what manner of love
the Father hath bestowed upon
us, that we should be called
the sons of God" (1 John 3:1).

THEREFORE I MAY BOLDLY SAY

I am

a person

of value.

ful worker. Help me to realize in humble adoration that I'm of value to You, Blessed Heavenly Father. In Jesus' name, amen.

Turning Insight Into Action

1. Expand Your Understanding

In a concordance look up the words *adoption* and *son.* Write down six references that speak of God's adopting us or the fact that we are sons of God. Write a statement of what it means to you to be an adopted child of God. How does this speak of your value, your worth to Him?

2. Search and Share

Think of what it means that God has called you His friend. To help clarify this in your mind write down five qualities you think of in a good friend. Then write down three traits of an unfaithful friend. Remember God has all the good qualities you appreciate in your best friend and more—so many more. Yet, God is not at all like the ones who disappoint or hurt others. Look up *friend* in a concordance and write down some of the qualities mentioned. Share with your friend, husband, wife what God's friendship is like as you have discovered in your study above.

3. Develop Your Awareness

Each morning this week repeat these precious truths to yourself as you begin your day.

"I am God's adopted child. He is my Heavenly Father."

"I am God's friend. He is my Friend."

"I am God's co-worker, partner in His world-saving enterprises."

Thank God for each of these privileges. Purpose to rehearse these thoughts several times during each day.

Thank Him again. Write out an example of how these thoughts brought encouragement and strength in a difficult situation. Share with your partner and/or friend(s).

4. Store Up God's Thoughts
"Behold, what manner of love the Father hath bestowed upon us, that we should be called the sons of God . . ." (1 John 3:1). Additional verses for memory— John 15:14, 15; Romans 8:15; 1 Corinthians 3:9.

5. Reach Out in Love
(a) This week write a letter to God telling Him how you feel about being His adopted child, being His friend, and being called of Him to work with Him in His world-saving, life-enriching ministries. Express your love and gratitude to Him.

(b) Under "Search and Share" you have listed five qualities of a good friend and the traits of an unfaithful friend. Pray for and then look for opportunities to demonstrate one or more of these qualities of a good friend to at least two people this week. These friendship deeds will give the person the vote of your friendship and help him to feel of value.

(c) To have friends one must show himself friendly (*see* Proverbs 18:24). This week especially practice being a cheerful, friendly person.

> Ask God to help you be that cheerful, friendly person.
>
> Practice looking at and smiling at people.
>
> Practice deliberately stopping and being friendly instead of hurrying on to the next duty. Show interest in another's activity by asking questions and listening.

Refrain from doing all the talking. Encourage others to talk about themselves, their views, their opinions, their achievements.

Take the initiative in building friendships. Introduce yourself. Call the other person by name.

(d) Write one or several examples of the good results of being friendly and cheerful.

(e) Check to see how much you convey to others, "I'm not interested in you."

Do you continue to watch TV or read when someone is talking to you about something that is important to them?

Do you turn away to other things or people when someone is talking to you?

Do you devote your whole attention to one person and exclude others?

One shared:

Upon being introduced to the woman next to me at a banquet, she said, "Glad to meet you," as she turned to another person and immediately began a conversation with him which lasted the whole evening. I felt like disappearing.

6. Sing the Truth

I'm of value made uniquely,
With a purpose that's divine.
God has given an assignment.
To bring glory to His Name.
How I praise Him, how I praise Him,
Called to glorify His Name,
Called to glorify His Name.

7
You Are Uniquely Designed

You did not just happen to come into being, nor did you just happen to be the sex you are or to have the physical features which you have. You, and all these special things about you, were planned in the mind of God long before you were ever born. He watched over you as you were being formed in the womb, and you became just as He planned.

I will praise thee; for I am fearfully and wonderfully made: marvellous are thy works; and that my soul knoweth right well. My substance was not hid from thee, when I was made in secret, and curiously wrought in the lowest parts of the earth.

Psalms 139:14, 15

God laid out a plan for your body structure and your person. No one else is exactly like you. You are uniquely designed—a very special person, a very special personality. You may be a very sensitive, quiet person or an aggressive, confident one. You may be a straight A student or a mediocre student, a creative thinker or a faithful, plodding type, a leader or a follower, an athletic type or poor in athletics.

God not only created you in the womb, He also continued to form you from that time. He is forming you, molding you in all the varying circumstances of life which He allows to touch you. He has a very special purpose for making you as you are. He made you the height you are, the temperament you are, the color you are. He gets the credit for every advantage you have had in life. He has given you certain strengths. He even allowed some "negative" things in your life through which you developed certain weaknesses. He wants you to use these strengths for Him and let your weaknesses work for Him and for you. Learn to "glory in your infirmities," not to hate or despise yourself because of them.

His Creative Design

You have been custom-made by a very wise almighty Creator. He has designed you very especially in every detail of your being. He is very excited over the tremendous possibilities for fulfilling His good purposes through this special person of His creative design.

Think of a human parallel for a moment. Envision an inventor who has produced a unique instrument to fulfill a special purpose and need. No one previously has designed something to fill this need in this unique way. How excited is the inventor! How he watches with careful attention as the instrument performs. How eagerly he will make any little adjustments to make the instrument more effective for its designed purpose. He tests, he tries, he sands, he chips areas of imperfection to make it perfectly suitable for its assigned job. He is filled with deep satisfaction and joy as the instrument begins to fulfill its designed purpose.

So the Lord, the God of this whole universe, has made you uniquely for a very special reason. He desires to give the world a special message through you. He has a unique job for you which no one has done or can possibly do. You are important to Him. He is excited about the prospects of your being happy, fulfilled, and satisfied. You will know this joyful fulfillment as you fully cooperate with Him and let Him fit you into the unique and special purpose for which He has designed you. And He who has designed you will be filled with joy and satisfaction when He sees you fulfilling the purpose for which He made you. He "delights" in us (*see* Isaiah 42:1).

Now it isn't as though He has merely an ultimate purpose in mind which should be realized out in some distant future. He has that. But His unique, ultimate purpose includes a process of growth. Each step is significant. Therefore, each day, each moment of your life is significant to Him. Oh, will you open your eyes wide to catch something of the vision of the important person you are to your Designer—the God of the whole universe? Will you catch a glimpse of His total adequacy to make you the joyful, fulfilled, useful person that He wants you to be and that you want to be?

Look From God's Perspective

Too long and too often we have failed to look at ourselves from God's perspective. We have been looking through other eyes. It may be we have been looking through the eyes of our own wrong self-evaluation— letting our sins, failures, mistakes fill our vision so that we have basically negative thoughts about ourselves. "I'm a failure." "I can't do anything right." "I'm a nobody." We may be looking through the eyes of our own dissatisfaction. We don't like the way we are made, or some physical weakness or impairment. We demean ourselves, hate ourselves. We feel inferior because of our looks, our limitations, our weaknesses. A Workshop lady shared:

> I've known something of this bitterness. I have resented my body, which is built like a bean pole with a set of crooked teeth near the top. But now I am able to truly praise God for the way He made me. As a result I now have more respect for the old frame. I take better care of it and even dress it up and keep it looking nicer.

We may be looking through envious eyes, longing to be like someone else. One girl said, "I was constantly trying to be like one of my friends, but since I found Psalm 139, I'm a different person. It's a joy to be myself!"

We may be looking through the eyes of others, family members and friends, who have belittled us or called us names. "Who do you think you are? You're nobody special!" We may have been compared unfavorably with others, or heard negative things said about us, as Martha:

> As I was growing up I remember longing so much for a loving family. It seemed my family was always trying to see how much they could hurt one another. Mom and Dad argued constantly, and Dad would often lash out at us kids in his anger, saying many things that he didn't mean. I will always remember Dad saying, at the height of his anger, that he wished he had put his five children in a gunnysack the day they were born and dropped them over a bridge. That was the popular method of getting rid of unwanted kittens, so it left quite an impression on me.

Long after I left home I was still blaming my parents and my background for my problems. I didn't get complete release from my bitter feelings until I could honestly thank God for giving me my family. I know now that I am much more sensitive to other people's feelings and need for love because of these experiences.

Whatever is the source, these attitudes of self-hatred and resentment are hindering you. Sometimes people think self-criticism is "spiritual" or "being humble." Instead, this attitude leads to unhappiness and defeat.

Accept Yourself as You Are

Instead of allowing these negative thoughts about looks, limitations, weaknesses, and failures, agree with God that the way He made you is okay with you. Instead of complaining to God, "Why have You made me this way?" or "Why did You allow this to happen to me?" you need to accept yourself as you are and the circumstances which have touched your life. The following steps taken meaningfully will bring real personal freedom and release.

Admit the wrong attitudes about yourself and toward God.

Ask God's forgiveness for your resentment and bitterness toward Him for making you that way or allowing the negative circumstances to touch you.

Thank God for these things you were resentful about.

Tell Him your desire to cooperate with Him in regard to whatever He wants to do in your life.

Make a total commitment to Him of all you are and everything you have.

Dedicate Your Weakness

Dedicate your weakness to Him. Talk to Him specifically about those weaknesses which tend to displease you most. Ask Him to take them and use them to be opportunities to show His strength.

And he said unto me, My grace is sufficient for thee: for my strength is made perfect in weakness. Most gladly therefore will I rather glory in my infirmities, that the power of Christ may rest upon me. Therefore I take pleasure in infirmities, in reproaches, in necessities, in persecutions, in distresses for Christ's sake: for when I am weak, then am I strong.

2 Corinthians 12:9, 10

Know that He wants to replace your weaknesses with His strength. Anticipate and observe occasions when He does. Give Him thanks. Let Him make your life one big adventure with Him as you find His grace sufficient in time of need. Dedicate to Him your strengths, abilities, gifts. Talk to Him specifically about these assets. Thank Him for each one. Ask Him to enable you by the power of the Holy Spirit to use them, not to gratify your own pride, but to magnify His great grace and to glorify His dear name.

It is true we also need to know our negative traits and shortcomings so that we can concentrate on improving these areas. But to *fix* our focus on these would encourage an enlarged negative image of ourselves and lead to self-concentration, discouragement, and defeat. Our focus must instead be fixed on what God has already done in our lives and what He yet intends to do. We must concentrate on the tremendous potential we have for this life, because He has, through redemption, made

us "partakers of the divine nature" (*see* 2 Peter 1:4). He
anticipates what this potential actually means for us as
He says that we are to "walk, even as he walked" (*see* 1
John 2:6), that is, to think, speak and act as Jesus did.
What a tremendous asset, what tremendous potential is
in our human frames because God, the Holy Spirit, is
there!

And how is this to be a real experience for me? By
abiding in Him. That is, making a confident, joyful, trust-
ful surrender of my whole being to His loving control. A
practical way of accomplishing this is to focus more and
more on the character of God and let Him do the work of
transforming me into His likeness. Make Him your emo-
tional focus.

Know that by His strength, by the power of the in-
dwelling Holy Spirit you have all that is essential to
realize your full potential. You have all that is necessary
to become the unique, special person He designed you
to be and to joyously fulfill His purpose.

Blessed Creator, My Heavenly Father, thank You for
making me the unique person that I am. How wise You
are to give me both weaknesses and strengths. I ac-
knowledge my many weaknesses and give them to You.
Use them for opportunities to make Your power and
strength clearly seen. I thank You for my strengths,
realizing they are precious gifts from You. I give them to
You, asking You to help me use them, not to gratify my
pride but to glorify Your name. In Jesus' name, amen.

Turning Insight Into Action

1. Expand Your Understanding
Study Psalms 139:13–16 and Isaiah 43:1, 7, 21. Jot
down four phrases which indicate you were designed by
God.

GOD HAS SAID

"I will praise thee; for I am fearfully
and wonderfully made: marvellous
are thy works; and that my soul
knoweth right well" (Psalms 139:14).

THEREFORE I MAY BOLDLY SAY

*I am
uniquely
designed.*

2. Search and Share

From Jeremiah 1:5–9 list two areas in which Jeremiah felt inadequate. What two things did Moses feel inferior and insecure about? (*See* Exodus 4:1–17.) Make a list of the things you do not like about yourself or feel inferior or insecure about. Be honest with the Lord and talk to Him about these things as Moses and Jeremiah did. Present them to Him and trust Him to strengthen you and use these things in a special way for His glory. Also list your assets and strengths. Commit them specifically to the Lord for His use to His glory.

Formulate a brief testimony of self-acceptance and be prepared to share, as the Lord gives opportunity, how you were released from bitterness and learned to accept the way God made you and the circumstances surrounding your life.

3. Develop Your Awareness

Ask someone who knows you well to write down three of your weaknesses and three of your strengths as he views you. Discuss the lists with him. Let it be a means of encouragement, challenge, growth. Ask that person to pray with you that God will use both your strengths and your weaknesses for His glory.

4. Store Up God's Thoughts

"I will praise thee; for I am fearfully and wonderfully made: marvellous are thy works; and that my soul knoweth right well" (Psalms 139:14).

Additional memory verses—Isaiah 43:7, 21.

5. Reach Out in Love

(a) Think back to how the Lord has comforted you in respect to a weakness. This week try to reach out in sensitivity to others and become aware of some possibly un*comfort*able areas and bring understanding and encouragement to them. To one who is quiet, timid, shy, commend her for her sweet smile, ability to listen, calmness. To one who has made a big blunder, commend him for other jobs well done.

Be very careful not to draw their attention to their weakness. Avoid such statements as: "Judy never says the right thing." "Tommy never seems to do anything right." "You're so quiet, don't you ever talk?" "Sally is so clumsy." "You really are a little mite." "She's a giant!"

(b) Take time to show your daughter or son how to do some jobs, such as: how to run the washer and dryer, how to crack eggs, how to line the garbage cans with a plastic bag, how to change the vacuum cleaner bag, how to answer the phone, how to make a bed, how to change a tire, how to mow the lawn, how to clear the table, how to sort the clothes, how to cut up and fry chicken. You will visibly see the self-worth developing in them as you patiently show them how and then take time to do it with them. (This could also apply to an employee and tasks he needs to learn.)

(c) As you have presented your weaknesses—disadvantages—to the Lord, specifically ask Him to use them this week to bring glory to His name. They might help you understand someone who is struggling with the same weakness and give you an opportunity to communicate comfort to him. Or through your weakness you may be more alert and sensitive to others with the same weakness. You can become God's intercessor for them and their need.

At our Workshop session in San Bernardino a lady asked, "Did you have a good night's rest, Verna? I prayed for a good rest for you." "Yes, I had a very good night's rest." Then she asked if I was especially tired yesterday during the long day of standing and speaking. I had to be honest and admit that I *was* unusually tired. She said, "I was thinking about you so much and prayed especially for your legs—standing so long." I was so thankful that the Lord had laid this on her heart and was thrilled to share with her, "It was my legs that were especially tired. I was wearing a new pair of shoes! I appreciate your sensitivity to me and to the Lord and especially appreciate your prayers and the strength He gave."

6. Sing the Truth

I'm of value made uniquely,
With a purpose that's divine.
God has given an assignment
To bring glory to His name.
How I praise Him, how I praise Him,
Called to glorify His Name,
Called to glorify His Name.

8
You Are Designed for a Purpose

"Why was I ever born?" "What am I here for anyway?" "What is the purpose for life and especially for my life?" Perhaps at times you have had these questions. Be deeply assured that God had a very special purpose for bringing you into this world, forming you, redeeming you, and making you His very own. You are uniquely designed for that special purpose. In Isaiah 43 God declares His ultimate purpose for you.

> . . . I have created him for my glory, I have formed him; yea, I have made him . . . . Ye are my witnesses, saith the Lord, and my servant whom I have chosen: that ye may know and believe me, and understand that I am he . . . . I, even I, am the Lord . . . . This people have I formed for myself; they shall shew forth my praise.
>
> Vv. 7, 10, 11, 21

You are one whom the only real God has chosen and purposed to show forth His character in your life. In order to do this, He says, "You will need to know Me, believe in Me, and understand that I am He, the only God." What a wonderful cause for living! The Lord, Jehovah, God Himself, made you for the purpose of knowing Him and showing others who He is and what He is like. The results are that you will experience the greatest possible joy, peace, and personal satisfaction and others will come to glorify His name. What a purpose! What higher purpose or calling could possibly be ours?

> Thus saith the Lord, Let not the wise man glory in his wisdom, neither let the mighty man glory in his might, let not the rich man glory in his riches: But let him that glorieth glory in this, that he understandeth and knoweth me, that I am the Lord which exercise loving-kindness, judgment, and righteousness, in the earth: for in these things I delight, saith the Lord.
>
> Jeremiah 9:23, 24

Jesus said, "And this is life eternal, that they might know thee the only true God, and Jesus Christ, whom thou hast sent" (John 17:3). The apostle Paul witnesses that this was the set purpose of his life, "That I may know him . . ." (Philippians 3:10).

To Know God Personally

Life *does* have a purpose. *Your* life has a purpose. That purpose is to come to know God personally and serve Him joyfully, bringing glory and praise to His name.

> The whole human race was created to glorify God and enjoy Him forever. Sin has switched the human race on to another track, but it has not altered God's purpose in the tiniest degree; and when we are born again we are brought into the realization of God's great purpose for the human race, viz., I am created for God, He made me.[4]

Oh, what a high calling, what a privilege—to know God, to serve Him, and to glorify Him! We can serve

Him acceptably and glorify Him only as we know Him.
God wants you to come to know Him personally, intimately. He wants you to know how much He loves you
and how much He cares for you. He wants you to know
that He is good, full of compassion, loving-kindness, and
mercy and is concerned for your personal well-being.
He is faithful and unchangeable. He wants you to know
that He tenderly yearns over and cares for you as a good
mother comforts and cares for her child. He wants you to
know that He cares for you when you are tempted, fearful, anxious, discouraged.

So we must conclude that our chief purpose and aim in
life must be to know God. Since we have been made for
God, real joy, peace, and fullness of life can be experienced only as we learn to know God. As we come to
know Him more intimately, more fully, we trust Him
more completely and are the more free from worries,
concerns, frustrations, anxieties. "And they that know
thy name will put their trust in thee . . ." (Psalms 9:10).
"Acquaint now thyself with him, and be at peace . . ."
(Job 22:21).

Think of it! The Almighty Creator, the Lord of Hosts,
God Himself wants you to be His personal, intimate
friend, and He wants to be your most intimate Friend.
The greatest encouragement, the greatest joy, the
greatest strength that can come to you is through an
awareness that He is there and that He loves, cares, and
has grace to help in time of need.

Take Definite Steps

Getting to know God requires involvement on your
part. You will need to take some definite steps.

1. Agree with Him—believe Him when He tells you
who you are in relationship to Him. "That ye may know

and *believe* me," He says. Realize you are of value, of worth to Him. Thank Him over and over for these precious truths. "Thank You, Father, that I am Your special treasure, that You have set Your love upon me, that You delight in Me."

2. Make a decisive and total commitment of your life to Him. Commit yourself fully to Him—His interests, His cause. "I delight to do thy will, O my God." "Thy will, not mine, be done." Totally integrate your life into His—accepting His will, His plans, His purposes, His ways, that your joy might be full. The Lord assumes full responsibility for the one who is entirely His.

3. Allow no sin to continue unchecked, unconfessed. "If I regard iniquity in my heart, the Lord will not hear me" (Psalms 66:18). Even in our human relationships, we cannot experience closeness to those whom we have offended. We need to continually exercise ourselves to have always a conscience void of offense toward God and toward men. "If we confess our sins, he is faithful and just to forgive us our sins, and to cleanse us from all unrighteousness" (1 John 1:9). Then we can again experience that closeness with Him and continue to grow in our relationship to Him and our knowledge of Him. The pure in heart shall see God (*see* Matthew 5:8).

4. Accept the trials and sufferings which He allows to touch you as opportunities to become more intimately acquainted with Him. It is through difficulties, trials, testings, sufferings, we tend to draw closer to Him. These afford opportunities for God's love, care, and grace to be manifested to us.

5. Meditate on who He is and what He promises to do for you. From your reading in preceding chapters, make a list of:

(a) Qualities which describe what God is like.

(b) What God promises to be to you.

(c) What God promises to do for you.

(d) Who He views you to be.

Review the lists systematically. Worship God for the Person that He is. Look for occasions when He is to you or does for you what He says. Thank Him for these occasions. Thank Him for how He views you.

6. Spend time with Him in His Word daily. Listen to Him as He speaks to you through His Word. Ask the Holy Spirit to help you put into practice what He says in His Word so that you know by life experience that it is true. It is better to read several verses, reread them, and assimilate the message than to read larger portions and get nothing to take with you.

7. Fellowship with Him through prayer. Let your prayer time be one of worship, confession, thanksgiving, and intercession, sharing with Him your needs, bringing your family and friends, your work, your responsibilities, your ministry before Him. It can be exciting to keep a prayer/praise notebook. In this you can keep your lists of qualities of God and His promises to you. Record your requests. Leave a space to record the date and way answered. Be definite in your requests. Taking the suggestion from Andrew Murray, I put at the top of my request pages, "I know what I have asked my Father, and I expect the answer."

So to know Him involves:

A commitment of will—knowing and doing the will of God.

A commitment of thought—thinking on, observing His person and His wondrous works, all that He is, all that He has done, and what He promises to do.

A commitment of time—fellowship in the Word and prayer.

A commitment of life—living for and unto Him, not unto self, not allowing sin to mar the fellowship.

Come to know Him as your Heavenly Father who is better than the grandest picture of an ideal father that you can possibly construct. As you increase in your knowledge of who He is, you will increase in joy, peace, satisfaction.

O Blessed Heavenly Father, I praise You for Your loving-kindness, goodness, faithfulness, mercy, and love. Thank You for making me for Yourself and desiring my life to be full of joy and peace. Help me to live with the one great concern of really, really knowing You, trusting You, and glorifying Your name here in this earth. By Your faithful Holy Spirit, work in and through me to accomplish this for Your glory. In Jesus' name, amen.

Turning Insight Into Action

1. *Expand Your Understanding*
Review the chapter. Study the following Scriptures: John 17:3; Jeremiah 9:23, 24; Isaiah 43:7, 10, 11, 21; Ephesians 1:6, 12, 14; Philippians 1:11. Try to write a simple, concise statement of God's purpose for your life.

2. *Search and Share*
As you read carefully through Isaiah 40:10–31, make a list of qualities and attributes of God. Try to find at least twelve. Write out two or three of God's promises to you in the same section. Share your findings with someone.

Or begin reading a book such as *The Knowledge of*

the Holy, by A. W. Tozer; *The God of All Comfort*, by
Hannah Whitall Smith; or *Knowing God*, by J. I. Packer,
to enlarge your understanding of who God is.

3. Develop Your Awareness

Daily this week review the list of attributes of God and
the promises He has made to you. Write out at least one
illustration of a situation in which God strengthened or
helped you as you meditated on thoughts of who God is.
Pray for at least one opportunity this week (and look for
God to give it) to share with someone how your knowledge of who God is and what He promises to do for you
gave you strength and encouragement to meet a difficult
situation.

4. Store Up God's Thoughts

"But let him that glorieth glory in this, that he understandeth and knoweth me, that I am the Lord which
exercise loving-kindness, judgment, and righteousness,
in the earth: for in these things I delight, saith the Lord"
(Jeremiah 9:24).

Additional verses for memory—John 17:3; Psalms
9:10; Job 22:21.

5. Reach Out in Love

People learn more of what God is like through seeing
His qualities demonstrated through our lives. Therefore,
think of several people whom you can encourage this
week.

(a) Let them know that they are important, of value,
and of worth by speaking words of appreciation to them,
giving them a smile, giving them a few minutes of your
time and attention, complimenting them on the way they
did something—their ideas, efforts.

(b) Share with someone what you discovered your

GOD HAS SAID

"But let him that glorieth glory in this,
that he understandeth and knoweth me,
that I am the Lord" (Jeremiah 9:24).

THEREFORE I MAY BOLDLY SAY

I am designed for a purpose.

purpose in life to be as you studied this chapter and the Scriptures mentioned.

(c) Write a letter or note of appreciation to a family member, or make a phone call giving a word of commendation, or make a special trip just to drop by to see them for a few minutes.

(d) Give your child/husband/wife an extra hug or kiss today. Or if this is not your regular habit, make sure you kiss them good night tonight. In some way, show them you care.

(e) When a friend or family member returns from an outing, a special event, or from a daily routine, take time to sit down and listen to them. Ask questions which express your interest. One woman shared how much it meant to her to have a listening mother.

When I got home from school, she was always there. Over a snack we would visit about the day's happenings. This made me *want* to go home, because I knew what I had done was important to her, and I wanted to share. Even later, after I came in from a date in high-school years, she would often get up when I got home, we'd have a cup of tea, and she would listen some more. It was never an interrogation. I *wanted* to share with her, because I knew she would listen and not preach or criticize or condemn. She really helped me solve my own problems by this listening without criticism and making me know she had faith in my ability to find the right solution.

(f) Make it a point today to have eye contact when you are talking to another or when someone speaks to you.

6. Sing the Truth

I'm of value made uniquely,
With a purpose that's divine.
God has given an assignment
To bring glory to His Name.
How I praise Him, how I praise Him.
Called to glorify His Name,
Called to glorify His Name.

9
You Are Given an Assignment

Who are you—*really?* Yes, you are one who is very special, one whom God dearly loves, one whom He has redeemed, one who has been fully accepted as a member of His family! You are of value, one who is uniquely designed, one who has purpose! But that isn't all yet! That is wonderful, but there is much more!

You have a very special assignment. You live in a world that needs changing. A world full of people with needs. They need to know who God is, what He is like. They need to know how much He loves them and what He desires to do for them. They need to know how much He wants to make them free from their guilt, their hostility, their fears. They need to know how they can be at peace with God, with themselves, and with others. You are His personal ambassador, representing Him, witnessing to them that He is the answer to these needs. Think of it! *You are a personal representative of the living God on assignment to make God visible to others around you.*

What a calling! What an assignment! What a purpose for living—making God visible to the people of your special world that they might be changed and God glorified! In this way they, too, will be able to fulfill God's purposes for them—to know Him and "to show forth His praise; to glorify His name" (*see* Isaiah 43:7, 21).

God's general plan (or goal) for you is that you become more and more like Jesus Christ (*see* Romans 8:29), in your manner, in your speech, and in your actions. He wants to show the people of your world what Jesus Christ is like, and He wants to do it through your life. ". . . that the life also of Jesus might be made manifest in our mortal flesh" (2 Corinthians 4:11). It's the life that expresses what Jesus Christ is really like that fulfills the purpose God has for you—to bring glory to His name. Therefore, He has given a very special assignment, a charge, a trust which is people related. In your daily life and work you're to demonstrate to others what Jesus Christ is really like. You're to love unconditionally as He loves. You're to be ministering comfort and encouragement instead of criticizing and belittling. You're to demonstrate His patience instead of your irritability in the midst of pressure.

In fact, as we communicate His love, kindness, and thoughtfulness to others, it's as though we are doing it unto Him. ". . . Inasmuch as ye have done it unto one of the least of these my brethren, ye have done it unto me" (Matthew 25:40). That is, when you fed the hungry, gave drink to the thirsty, clothed the naked, visited the sick and imprisoned, you did it for Him. Even the one who gives a child a cold drink of water in His name shall be rewarded (*see* Matthew 10:42). People and their needs are important to Jesus and they must be to us also. We should think of these occasions as opportunities to communicate His love to them.

Specific Job Assignments

In addition to this general assignment to demonstrate what Jesus Christ is really like, He has also given to each of us specific job assignments and special abilities to accomplish these particular jobs. This job assignment will take on different forms during different phases or stages of our lives. Each particular job assignment is very important to the total program of what God is accomplishing in His vast world. It is important that we do not diminish the value of our job or the job of another. It is also important that we not feel constantly dissatisfied with our job assignment and wish we had that of another. Each person is important and each is an important part of the whole. Each job assignment is important, just as the function of each member of the body is necessary to the good health of our physical being.

If the whole body were an eye, where were the hearing? If the whole were hearing, where were the smelling? . . . And the eye cannot say unto the hand, I have no need of thee: nor again the head to the feet, I have no need of you.

1 Corinthians 12:17, 21

One's job description might be to baby-sit, to teach, to do custodial work, to preach, to be a waitress, a maid, an engineer, a factory worker, a doctor, a mother, a wife, a husband. Whatever form the job description takes doesn't really matter. The essential thing is to be faithful in doing a job well, doing it as unto the Lord, and while doing it, manifesting the qualities of the life of Jesus. God has purposely created us with different abilities and gifts so that we might fulfill the specific assignments to which He calls us. Our assignments are people related and in them we are to encourage one another and to help each other grow. Provoke (stimulate) one another unto love and to good works (*see* Hebrews 10:24). We are to use our special gifts and abilities in this way.

Job Size and Shape

Now it is true that God always calls us to a job that is much, much bigger than we are—far beyond our natural abilities. He does this so that we will realize how very much we need to depend on His supernatural grace and power to accomplish it. We must remember that our real capacity is not measured by our natural abilities but by the supernatural power of God working in and through us. Therefore, though we are not the same *size* as the job, we are the same *shape.* He gives us the kind of abilities and gifts that are suitable to our particular assignment— that particular sphere of service to which He has called us. We are the same general shape, but not the size. He doesn't put a square peg in a round hole. Instead, the round peg goes into the round hole but the hole is far, far too big for the peg to fit. We are far too small to fill the position, except by His supernatural work in us. "Without me," Jesus said, "ye can do nothing" (*see* John 15:5). But, "I can do all things [related to His assignment, His will for me] through Him who strengthens me" (Philippians 4:13 NAS).

God does not leave us to ourselves or to our own resources to accomplish His assignments. As God says, we are ". . . workers together with him . . ." (2 Corinthians 6:1). We are cooperators with God Himself. I am full of power by the Spirit of the Lord to do all the will of God and thereby fulfill His assignments to me. It is God Almighty working in us both to will and to do of His good pleasure (*see* Philippians 2:13). We are "Strengthened with all might, according to his glorious power, unto all patience and longsuffering with joyfulness" (Colossians 1:11).

GOD HAS SAID

"This people have I formed for myself;
they shall shew forth my praise"
(Isaiah 43:21).

THEREFORE I MAY BOLDLY SAY

*I am
given
an assignment.*

Think Big

Think *large* thoughts of God and what He can accomplish through you. Of yourself, you can't. But that's not the whole story. Linked with the Almighty you can! He has made big promises for which He is totally adequate. William Carey caught this essential principle when he said, "Expect great things from God; attempt great things for God." Too frequently we have feared pride and have settled back feeling—we aren't important, our work isn't important, we're nobody with nothing significant to do or be. So we settle for low achievement, obscurity, and defeat and call it humility, when all the time God is waiting for us, by faith, to allow His bigness to be linked to our smallness. Then we can make a distinctly positive impression for His glory in our special worlds of His choosing and with the contacts of His assignments. Let your mind dwell on the promises of God and fill your thoughts with images of what you can become and accomplish. Certainly the Christian, above all people, should be able to "think big" because we are linked to a big God who has promised big things.

May you have as your life's goal to know Him and to glorify Him so that you, too, at the end can say with Jesus, "Father . . . . I have glorified thee on the earth: I have finished the work which thou gavest me to do" (John 17:1, 4).

Heavenly Father, thank You that You have given me an assignment. Thank You for the wonderful privilege of being Your personal representative here on this earth. Thank You that You have sent me to demonstrate what You are really like. Make me more like Jesus—having His joy, His love, His understanding, His patience, His calm, His meek and quiet spirit.

*In all attitudes and actions make me like Jesus Christ
that I might glorify Your name. I don't want my life to
be wasted or useless. I do want it to really count for
You. Here are my hands, my mouth, my mind, my feet,
my life. Take me, use me as You desire. In Jesus' name,
amen.*

Turning Insight Into Action

1. Expand Your Understanding

From the chapter content and especially from the following Scriptures, formulate a summary statement indicating the general overall assignment God has given to
you. Remember, this is a lifelong assignment.

Romans 8:29
2 Corinthians 4:7–11
Isaiah 43:7, 21

2. Search and Share

Think through and jot down the special roles and job
assignments God has given you at this particular time in
your life. Beside each write specific things you can do to
fulfill your general, lifelong assignment in respect to
each of these. For example, as a mother you might list,
"Being patient, gracious, loving with my husband and
children." Write down some specific things you must be
careful to avoid doing in order to fulfill the general assignment God has given. Discuss both of these lists with
another (spouse, friend) and add to both lists from your
sharing time.

3. Develop Your Awareness

This week notice what your general attitude or response is when someone wants you to do something for
them or with them. Is there evidence of a servant's

heart—"Whatever there is to do, I'll do it"—without consideration for whether it is a menial or an honorable task? Is your response characterized by gladness and joy? "And whatsoever ye do, do it heartily, as to the Lord . . ." (Colossians 3:23). "Serve the Lord with gladness . . ." (Psalms 100:2). Remember, Jesus says you are serving Him when you serve one of "the least of these." Is your attitude one of, "I'll be glad to"?

4. Store Up God's Thoughts

"This people have I formed for myself; they shall shew forth my praise" (Isaiah 43:21).

Additional memory verses—2 Corinthians 4:11; Matthew 25:40.

5. Reach Out in Love

(a) This week give special attention to practicing unselfishly considering the other person's ideas. When your husband, child, friend, fellow worker comes up with an idea for something to do or a different method for doing the job before you, respond with, "Yes, let's do it," or "Oh, that would be fun," or "Great idea," or "I think we should try that," or "Let's plan how we can put that idea into practice."

(b) This week give special attention to practicing the attitude of the servant's heart—serving with cheerfulness. When someone asks you to do something for them, respond with, "I'll be glad to."

(c) Offer to do a little favor for a family member or friend—cut their hair, sew up a hem, fix a broken toy, repair a faucet.

(d) One woman shared:

As a teacher of second graders I wanted to check myself on the amount of attention each child was receiving personally. I wrote each name on a chart and for two weeks I recorded a mark by the child's name for each hug, correction, praise, and so forth. I tried not to read my record until the end of the two weeks. At the completion of the second week I was sad to see the names of the children who had not received any personal attention from me. The aggressive, demanding type received attention, the precocious, winning type had received attention, but the precious, quiet ones in the middle were overlooked. It takes time to keep the record, but what a tremendous tool to use in not overlooking the needs of each one God has placed in my care.

Plan to incorporate this idea as a check in your family or your classroom.

(e) Ask a friend or family member for his choice of an activity to do together this week. Make plans to include that in your schedule. You might find an interesting surprise awaiting you; as one Workshop lady shared,

> My husband asked that the children and I go with him to pick up his new tractor. When I heard it meant getting the family up and out at 5:00 A.M., I wasn't so sure this was a good idea! But I decided to be enthusiastic about this venture that meant so much to him. He really enjoyed making it a family adventure and it turned out to be fun for all of us. The kids were thrilled to ride in the big diesel truck, and we all got to see the sunrise together. As a bonus, afterward my husband took us out for breakfast—a rare and special treat!

6. Sing the Truth

> I'm of value made uniquely,
> With a purpose that's divine.

God has given an assignment
To bring glory to His Name.
How I praise Him, how I praise Him,
Called to glorify His Name,
Called to glorify His Name.

10

You Are Continually Sustained

The Lord does not leave His children to their own resources to get along "somehow." Instead, He continually sustains! To say that He will sustain you means that He is ready to give you the aid, the support, the encouragement, the comfort you need. He will strengthen your spirit and carry the weight of your burdens. He will uphold you, nourish you, provide for you, bear you up, and strengthen you. He expresses this in so many ways.

The Lord upholdeth all that fall, and raiseth up all those that be bowed down.

Psalms 145:14

The eternal God is thy refuge, and underneath are the everlasting arms . . . .

Deuteronomy 33:27

He giveth power to the faint; and to them that have no might he increaseth strength.

Isaiah 40:29

But they that wait upon the Lord shall renew their strength; they shall mount up with wings as eagles; they shall run, and not be weary; and they shall walk, and not faint.

Isaiah 40:31

Fear thou not; for I am with thee: be not dismayed; for I am thy God: I will strengthen thee; yea, I will help thee; yea, I will uphold thee with the right hand of my righteousness.

Isaiah 41:10

More Than Enough

He promises to be to us whatever we need. He continually encourages: "Come unto Me" (*see* Matthew 11:28); "Look to Me" (*see* Isaiah 45:22); "And therefore will the Lord wait, that He may be gracious unto you . . ." (Isaiah 30:18). What is your need?

> PATIENCE? He is the God of patience (*see* Romans 15:5).
>
> LOVE? He is the God of Love (*see* 2 Corinthians 13:11).
>
> ENCOURAGEMENT? He is the God of consolation (*see* Romans 15:5).
>
> HOPE? He is the God of hope (*see* Romans 15:13).
>
> PEACE? He is the God of peace (*see* Hebrew 13:20).
>
> COMFORT? He is the God of all comfort (*see* 2 Corinthians 1:3).
>
> POWER? He is the Almighty God (*see* 2 Corinthians 6:18).
>
> MERCY? God is rich in mercy (*see* Ephesians 2:4).
>
> FORGIVENESS? He is the God who forgives (*see* Hebrews 8:12).
>
> STRENGTH? He is the all-sufficient God (*see* 2 Corinthians 12:9).
>
> HELP? God is your helper (*see* Psalms 54:4).

This list could go on and on. He is *El Shaddai*—the God who is more than enough! "For this God is our God

for ever and ever: he will be our guide even unto death"
(Psalms 48:14).

Behold your God! Think upon Him. Consider who He
is who promises to sustain you, who continually invites
you to come to Him and find Him to be whatever you
need. What attention He gives you. How precious you
are to Him that He waits to be gracious to you. He loves
you and wants to give you inner rest and peace.

> Come to Me, all you who labor and are heavy-laden and
> over burdened, and I will cause you to rest—I will ease
> and relieve and refresh your souls. Take My yoke upon
> you, and learn of Me; for I am gentle (meek) and humble
> (lowly) in heart, and you will find rest—relief, ease and
> refreshment and recreation and blessed quiet—for your
> souls. For My yoke is wholesome (useful, good)—not
> harsh, hard, sharp or pressing, but comfortable, gracious
> and pleasant; and My burden is light and easy to be
> borne.
>
> Matthew 11:28-30 AMPLIFIED

This One not only looks upon you with understanding
and empathy, but He is there to help, to sustain in every
time of varied need. Therefore you can boldly, confidently come and "Cast thy burden upon the Lord, and
He shall sustain thee: he shall never suffer the righteous
to be moved" (Psalms 55:22). As you release the full
weight of your burden upon Him, you will find Him
there. You will find Him adequate for you in the midst of
that need. He will sustain you.

> For we do not have a High Priest Who is unable to
> understand and sympathize and have a fellow feeling
> with our weaknesses and infirmities and liability to the

assaults of temptation, but One Who has been tempted in every respect as we are, yet without sinning.

Hebrews 4:15 AMPLIFIED

Accept His gracious invitation and come boldly to His throne of grace and find grace to help in time of need.

Let us then fearlessly and confidently and boldly draw near to the throne of grace—the throne of God's unmerited favor [to us sinners]; that we may receive mercy [for our failures] and find grace to help in good time for every need—appropriate help and well-timed help, coming just when we need it.

Hebrews 4:16 AMPLIFIED

Bruised and Struggling

F. B. Meyer speaks so warmly of God's tender sustaining grace:

Now, troubled soul, look unto these words. ". . . I am thy God" (Isaiah 41:10). They are spoken by one who cannot lie, and spoken for thee. They are as much meant for thee as though they had never been claimed by another; and God is prepared to fulfill them in thy life to the brim. He is thy God, and will never act unworthily of thy trust. Where thou art weakest and most easily overcome, He will strengthen thee. Where thou needest help, He will give His, so that thy difficult task shall be easily mastered. And when thou art too weary to walk; when no more strength remains in thee; when thou sinkest on the battlefield or the steep hill—He will uphold thee. Weakness, weariness, and sin, never fail to draw forth the deepest sympathy from the Lord Jesus. Nothing lays a stronger hold upon Him, or brings Him more swiftly to our side. At home our mother was always sweet but sweetest when we were ill or weary. Christ's love is like mother's. Those who are most bruised and struggling get the tenderest manifestations of His love. He resembles the strong man, with muscles like iron, and who stands like a rock, but who will bend in tears and tenderness over his cripple-child.[5]

As you find Him totally adequate for your total need, then you will be able to minister to others who need comfort and encouragement. Study carefully how He has sustained or is sustaining you in a need. Make notes on the steps you have taken to appropriate His grace, encouragement, strength. Store this up in your heart and mind. Ask the Lord to give you opportunity to share with someone who also needs His comfort. Preparing to pass on to others the way you have been sustained and comforted will result in a double blessing to you. It will help you focus your attention on your blessings rather than difficulties, and it will help you to become useful in a ministry to others which gives purpose to life. You live in a world of people who need such a message. God wants to use you to help meet their needs. Then you will realize more fully that you are of worth to Him and to them.

Blessed [be] the God and Father of our Lord Jesus Christ, the Father of sympathy (pity and mercies) and the God [Who is the Source] of every consolation and comfort and encouragement; Who consoles and comforts and encourages us in every trouble (calamity and affliction), so that we may also be able to console (comfort and encourage) those who are in any kind of trouble or distress, with

GOD HAS SAID

"Cast thy burden upon the Lord,
and he shall sustain thee"
(Psalms 55:22).

THEREFORE I MAY BOLDLY SAY

*I am
continually
sustained.*

the consolation (comfort and encouragement) with which we ourselves are consoled and comforted and encouraged by God.

2 Corinthians 1:3, 4 AMPLIFIED

Comfort ye, comfort ye my people, saith your God.

Isaiah 40:1

Blessed God of comfort and of peace, thank You for continually drawing me close to Yourself, showing me more of who You really are and how much You want to continually sustain me. Help me always to come boldly to Your throne of grace and find that grace to help in time of need. Thank You that You are El Shaddai—One more than adequate for my needs. Praise, praise to You! In Jesus' name, amen.

Turning Insight Into Action

1. Expand Your Understanding
Read again the promises the Lord gives in Psalms 145:14 and Isaiah 41:10. Look up in a dictionary the words which tell us what He promises to do for us. Write out these words with their synonyms. Expand the meaning of the verses to include these ideas as you reread the verses. From your study write down one thought which gives special comfort to you.

2. Search and Share
As you review the chapter, jot down three thoughts regarding what God promises to do for you. Ask yourself why these thoughts are especially meaningful to you. Share with a family member or with a friend.

During this week observe and write down specific times when the Lord sustained you through His Word or through another person. Think of a time when He gave you strength in weakness, enabled you to be patient in a trying situation, gave encouragement through His Word or another person at a time of discouragement, gave your heart rest and peace in a frustrating circumstance.

3. *Develop Your Awareness*

Think through your experiences and write down three ways another person has brought encouragement, hope, strength, comfort, expression of love to you. Recall what a help it was. It might be something like this Vacation Bible School superintendent shared:

> Quite tired and discouraged, I was thinking to myself, "I don't know why I try to do things like this. Next year I'm sure going to find someone else to do it!" Right then one of the teachers came and put her arm around me and said, "We sure appreciate you, do you know it?" Those few words of encouragement seemed to take away all the tired feelings and give me new zeal and enthusiasm to get in and work harder and plan bigger.

Write down the names of people to whom you could give the same kind of encouragement, hope, comfort, expressions of love. God sustains, comforts us that we might in turn give the same kind of comfort and strong sympathy to others in their times of trial and distress (*see* 2 Corinthians 1:3–5). Choose one or more of the projects listed under "Reach Out in Love."

4. *Store Up God's Thoughts*

"Cast thy burden upon the Lord, and he shall sustain thee . . ." (Psalms 55:22).

Additional memory verses—Hebrews 4:16; 2 Corinthians 12:9; Isaiah 41:10.

5. *Reach Out in Love*

(a) Copy a meaningful verse of Scripture or a para-
graph from a devotional book for someone who is sick or
going through a trial. Send it through the mail along with
an explanatory note: "This has been so very helpful to
me. Trust it will be an encouragement to you, too."

(b) Plan to smile at each member of your family every
morning this week. (Do it, even if you don't feel like it!)

(c) If someone is leaving home for a short or long trip,
slip some little notes or presents into the traveler's suit-
cases. Something like, "I love you," or "Hurry home,"
and so forth will make that person feel loved and remembered.

(d) Thank someone today for little things like carrying
in the groceries, mailing some letters for you, checking
the oil in your car.

(e) Express confidence in someone today. Be sensitive to any area of insecurity and encourage them in that
area.

(f) From any hymnbooks available to you, find several
hymns which communicate this truth of God's sustaining grace. (Many hymnbooks provide subject indexes.)
Sing the hymns together with several others this week.
Memorize one that is especially meaningful.

6. *Sing the Truth*

> I'm so weak, but He sustains me,
> Gives me strength for every day.
> My Companion every moment,
> He is with me all the way.
> How I praise Him, how I praise Him,
> For His presence and His strength,
> For His presence and His strength.

11

You Are Accompanied by God

One of the greatest comforts which can come to an individual is the presence of a loving, understanding, supporting companion. If the relationship is a deep one, many times in the face of sorrow or difficulty just to know the person is "there" is adequate—even though the exchange of words might be few.

The presence of a father who has a loving, caring relationship with his son is such a comfort to his son who is in distress. His very presence brings strength, quiets fears, gives hope. The closer the relationship, the greater the comfort his presence brings.

Just so for the redeemed child of God, the greatest source of encouragement and strength in the midst of distressing, frustrating, fearful situations is a fresh realization of the presence of our Heavenly Father. The degree of rest (comfort) and strength one receives depends on the Christian's closeness to the Person of God and his understanding of the character of our Heavenly Father. This is why Paul prays for the Ephesian Christians that they would be ". . . rooted and grounded in love . . . . And to know the love of Christ, which passeth knowledge, that ye might be filled with all the fulness of God" (Ephesians 3:17, 19).

Throughout the Scriptures there are numerous examples of God strengthening His people, comforting them, dispelling their fears, and bringing them to a quiet, restful trust in Him—simply by reminding them of His presence with them.

"I Am With You"

Jesus said to the disciples in the midst of the storm, ". . . it is I; be not afraid" (Matthew 14:27). The Great Commission gives assurance of His unending presence: ". . . lo, I am with you alway, even unto the end . . ." (Matthew 28:20). Jesus' very name, Emmanuel, means "God with us" (*see* Matthew 1:23). The great affirmation of Hebrews 13:5 is: ". . . I will never leave thee, nor forsake thee."

When God called Moses to that seemingly impossible task of bringing the children of Israel out from under Pharaoh's reign, the greatest word of strength and assurance He could give Moses was: ". . . Certainly I will be with thee . . ." (Exodus 3:12).

When Moses was about to depart from this life, he gathered all Israel together to encourage them to be fearless and courageous: ". . . for the Lord thy God, he it is that doth go with thee; he will not fail thee, nor forsake thee" (Deuteronomy 31:6). Moses then talked personally to the one who was to be the new leader, Joshua, and again used the same words of strong encouragement. "And the Lord . . . will be with thee, he will not fail thee, neither forsake thee: fear not, neither be dismayed" (Deuteronomy 31:8).

After Moses died and Joshua became the leader, God again personally used these same words to encourage and strengthen Joshua. ". . . I will be with thee: I will not fail thee, nor forsake thee . . . . the Lord thy God is with thee whithersoever thou goest" (Joshua 1:5, 9).

God, through Isaiah, again gives this same word to His children: "Fear thou not; for I am with thee . . ." (Isaiah 41:10).

The words the Lord used to answer Jeremiah's fears of

the people and his personal inadequacy for the job God called him to do were simply, "Be not afraid . . . I am with thee [and will enable you to do what is necessary in fulfilling My plan for you]" (*see* Jeremiah 1:8).

There are no more potent words to bring the fearful heart to rest, to motivate the inadequate one to be strong and courageous, to bring faith, hope, confidence to the discouraged one than these simple words, "I am with you."

When you realize God is there with you—what a difference! Especially when you realize who it is that is with you and what He is really like. He uses human relationships to help us understand who He is and what He wants to be to us. Earlier we considered that we are His adopted children. He is our Heavenly Father—all and much more than any "perfect" earthly father could be. He calls us His friends, and wants to be our Friend—more than the dearest of earthly friends. He says, "You are My people, and I am your God—the Almighty, ever-loving, all-powerful, infinite, eternal God. The One who is in Himself love, goodness, mercy, wisdom, faithfulness, truthfulness, justice. God, the Lord of Hosts—leader of all the armies of Heaven and earth. *El Shaddai*—the God who is more than enough!"

It is He that is with us and in us! It is He who is totally adequate for our total need. The only thing necessary to link His adequacy with our need is a vital commitment to Him and an active faith in Him.

The Holy Spirit Within You

Not only is He *with* you, but He dwells *in* you. He has taken up residence within you by the Holy Spirit. "What? know ye not that your body is the temple of the

GOD HAS SAID

"Be not afraid, neither be thou dismayed:
for the Lord thy God is with thee
whithersoever thou goest"
(Joshua 1:9).

THEREFORE I MAY BOLDLY SAY

*I am
accompanied
by God.*

Holy Ghost which is in you ? . . ." (1 Corinthians 6:19).
He says, ". . . I will dwell in them, and walk in them
. . ." (2 Corinthians 6:16). "Know ye not that ye are the
temple of God, and that the Spirit of God dwelleth in
you?" (1 Corinthians 3:16).

Not only has He come to live in us who are His redeemed children, but we are continually to be filled
with the Holy Spirit, that His life might be manifest
through our lives—His love, His joy, His peace, longsuffering, gentleness, goodness, faith, meekness, tem-
perance (*see* Galatians 5:22, 23).

Ephesians 5:19–21 indicates that as we are letting
Him fill us and manifest His life through us, there will
be a singing, rejoicing heart, a thankful, grateful attitude,
and a meek, humble spirit. There will be the melody in
our hearts of giving thanks and submitting one to
another.

Practice His Presence

Learn to cultivate His friendship, His companionship.
Begin to "practice His presence." Each morning in your
first waking moments establish the thought of His presence with you. Thank Him that He is there and will be
with you all the day. Thank Him, too, that He lives
within. Ask for a fresh infilling of the Holy Spirit for your
life and work today. Thank Him that He has filled you.
Look for evidences of the fruit of the Holy Spirit as He
undertakes to produce them in you as you cooperate
with Him.

Oh, my dear reader, I could not give you any more
encouraging words than these. *Know that He is there
with you and will go with you all the way.* A fresh
awareness of His presence with you will give you peace
in the midst of turmoil, power for your weakness, cour-

age for your difficulties, strength for your inadequacies,
rest from your fears. He is there with you. By faith take
hold of His almightiness for your present need.

He is able and ready to deliver you, to give you
strength and courage to face that difficult or impossible
situation, to give you patience, to put His words in your
mouth, to fully enable you for whatever He calls you to
do or to be.

What an honor to have Him as my constant
companion—the God of the universe, my Creator, my
Redeemer. The Lord of Hosts, the Almighty One, my
loving Heavenly Father is my Counselor, my Guide, my
Friend. What an incentive to purposeful living to realize
that to Him I'm of value, and He desires my fellowship,
my companionship.

*Blessed Heavenly Father, how I praise and adore You
for Your faithfulness, for Your unchangeableness, for
Your goodness, mercy, and love. Praise, praise to You
that You want to be my constant companion. I know
that I have not merited the privilege, but I accept Your
invitation. Forgive me for my frequent unfaithfulness.
Thank You that You remain faithful. Thank You that
You are with me always. Thank You for the Holy Spirit,
who lives within me. Fill me afresh today—Your love,
joy, peace, power—all that I need for today. I pray in
Jesus' name, amen.*

Turning Insight Into Action

1. Expand Your Understanding

Using some specific phrases from the verses mentioned and the thoughts given in this chapter, write
three statements affirming the fact of God's presence

with you. Also write three statements describing who it is that is present with you.

2. *Search and Share*

Think of a special time in your life when a fresh awareness of God's presence brought you courage, comfort, or quieted your fears. Write out the incident. Share with another person how this truth has affected your thinking and your reactions to life's problems.

3. *Develop Your Awareness*

This week, in a special way concentrate on practicing God's presence. During your first waking moments establish the thought of His presence. Talk with Him, "Thank You, Blessed Lord, that You are with me now and will be with me throughout this day. Help me always to remember You are there." Anticipate His presence throughout the day. Write an illustration of how you were reminded of His presence and experienced peace.

4. *Store Up God's Thoughts*

". . . be not afraid, neither be thou dismayed: for the Lord thy God is with thee whithersoever thou goest" (Joshua 1:9).

Additional verses for memory—Isaiah 41:10; Hebrews 13:5, 6; Joshua 1:5; Deuteronomy 31:8.

5. *Reach Out in Love*

Think of someone who needs the comfort of your presence this week. There are no doubt many around you who feel as one expressed, "Most of the time I feel God is busy somewhere else." Giving of your time and your presence to another can be a big step for them to realize God is *not* busy somewhere else. He is a "very present help."

(a) Take time with someone in your own family who needs the quiet assurance of your presence and love. It may be he needs you to listen to him. Or, it might be a fun activity, or help with a project. A mother shared how her two-year-old son obviously wants the comfort of her presence:

> Even if he can see I'm occupied, he will come up, grab my hand, and say, "Mommy, come on!" Then he leads me into the den where he has his blocks all ready for us to play. I always try to give him a little time, even if I am busy, since he obviously is expressing a need to have me near.

(b) If someone you know is grieving over a lost loved one, plan to visit them. Even if you don't have many words, give them the comfort of your presence. If a visit is impossible, make a phone call or send a note. Share with them the comfort of the Lord.

(c) Share your memorization project for this week with three people. Let them know how the verse (or verses) has helped you to be more conscious of God's presence with you.

(d) Plan to visit someone who is alone—a widow, a wife whose husband is gone much of the time, a single person who lives alone, an elderly person, someone in the hospital or nursing home.

(e) Plan an outing for someone who is alone much of the time. It could be a picnic, or a walk through the park, a stroll on a mall, lunch together, a concert, an evening of games at your home.

6. Sing the Truth

> I'm so weak, but He sustains me,
> Gives me strength for every day.
> My Companion every moment,
> He is with me all the way.
> How I praise Him, how I praise Him,
> For His presence and His strength,
> For His presence and His strength.

12
You Are God's Responsibility

Oh, what wonder! How amazing! The Lord of Hosts, the Lord of all the armies in Heaven and on earth has called me to Himself, and I have the privilege of being vitally involved with Him as He works in this earth to accomplish His purposes in individuals, in families, in nations—to the glory of His name. Now crown that with this additional wonder! As I am totally committed to His will for my life, He assumes full responsibility for me—for my own personal needs, for the outcome of the projects He assigns to me, for the effectiveness of the ministry, for the response of the people, for the fruit of the labor, and for the permanency of the work.

Listen to Me . . . you who have been borne by Me from birth . . . Even to your old age, I shall be the same, And even to your graying years I shall bear you ! . . .
                                        Isaiah 46:3, 4 NAS

. . . I will be to them a God, and they shall be to me a people.
                                        Hebrews 8:10

These precious words from the living God to whom we belong give us the confident assurance that He assumes full responsibility for us.

He assumes responsibility for the way I was made and

the way I developed through environment and circumstances. Some things have come to us by God's ap-
pointment, others He has permitted. You were born with
a particular temperament. You were born of particular
parents in a unique home situation and social environment. He permitted you to begin life with certain disadvantages or infirmities. He made; He will bear.

Of course, there are some things for which we are
largely responsible. Many times through habits of sin
and selfishness we have distorted our original makeup.
For these things we must not blame God or say that He
is responsible but rather look to Him for forgiveness and
victory to overcome. Or if there is a continuing resultant
weakness, then we must trust Him to use that weakness
for His glory. Even in these things He does not leave us
to ourselves or forsake us, but He will bear with us. Our
innate weaknesses which result from our sins or failures
are all the more reason to cast ourselves and our circumstances upon Him. He will assume responsibility to
give His all-sufficient grace for my weaknesses, and His
power will enable me to use my innate and acquired
strengths for Him. As I cooperate with Him, He will see
to it that both in my weaknesses and strengths I will
bring glory to His name.

His Potter's Vessel

As in every circumstance and situation I trustingly
yield to Him, He assumes the responsibility of making
me more and more like Jesus Christ—His ultimate goal
for my life character. I am His workmanship (*see* Ephesians 2:10), His garden under cultivation (*see* Isaiah
58:11), His potter's vessel (*see* Jeremiah 18:1–6). As I
yield willingly to Him, I become as clay in the hands of
the Potter, and He assumes responsibility for the out-

come of the product. He will continue His faithful work and successfully complete it.

> Being confident of this very thing, that he which hath begun a good work in you will perform it until the day of Jesus Christ.
>
> Philippians 1:6

Oh may you and I be increasingly, unreservedly, always, only His—by perpetual personal consent, that we might experience the overflowing joy, peace, and fulfillment that comes in relaxing confidently in His goodness and faithfulness.

As I am entirely His, not only does He faithfully work in me to develop Christlike qualities, but He assumes responsibility to work for my good through circumstances and situations He allows to touch me (*see* Romans 8:28). Perhaps even now you are going through testings, trials which seem too much to bear. Circumstances may seem to indicate to you that God has forgotten or that He doesn't care. It may even be He allowed you to be united in a marriage that *seems* not to be for your best interests or even His best interests. It may be you have a wayward child for whom you feel at least in part responsible because of your lack of knowledge or ability to meet his needs. It may be an accident has occurred—perhaps even through your thoughtlessness. Or perhaps this is a time when things are more difficult than you expected. For the trusting heart, godly character is forged in the fire, the flood, the darkness. ". . . when he hath tried me, I shall come forth as gold" (Job 23:10). He assumes responsibility to be faithful to us and to His promises. He will cause even trials to work out for your personal good and for His glory.

God does not withdraw Himself from us when we find ourselves in difficult, hard-to-understand trials. Nor does He withdraw Himself from us in hard situations which are the result of our own selfishness, willfulness, thoughtlessness, or ignorance in the past. He remains faithful to us and simply invites us to come confidently to Him and obtain grace to help in time of need.

Strength in Temptation

He assumes the responsibility of not allowing me to be tempted more than I am able to bear by His grace.

There hath no temptation taken you but such as is common to man: but God is faithful, who will not suffer you to be tempted above that ye are able; but will with the temptation also make a way to escape, that ye may be able to bear it.

1 Corinthians 10:13

God does not plan to keep us from temptation, but He promises to strengthen us in the midst of the temptation and help us through it.

Through temptation we realize afresh our need of Him. As we use this opportunity to draw upon His grace and power, it can actually be a benefit to us, a means of growing in godly character. Through temptation we learn more about ourselves—our weaknesses and our needs. We should use the occasion to rely upon His strength. Each victory over temptation gives the over-comer new strength and a new humility and joy which comes from a fresh awareness of the presence and power of God.

God assumes the responsibility to supply all my needs (Philippians 4:19). As I am walking in obedience to Him I have the privilege of claiming His wonderful promises.

> But seek ye first the kingdom of God, and his righteousness; and all these things shall be added unto you.
>
> Matthew 6:33

> Be anxious for nothing, but in everything by prayer and supplication with thanksgiving let your requests be made known to God.
>
> Philippians 4:6 NAS

He amplifies this to us in Matthew 6:24–34. He further affirms this when He refers to Himself as the great "I AM." It's as though He is saying, "I AM _____," leaving the blank for us to fill in. "I AM" whatever you need. "I AM strength in weakness, joy in sorrow, help in time of need, wisdom for decision making, comfort in trouble, guidance in perplexity, peace in the midst of conflict, courage in fearfulness. I AM whatever you need. As a blank check, fill in the details, draw upon Me. Call upon Me. Come to Me—the unchanging, ever-loving One. I will give you whatever you need."

The Fruit Is His

God assumes responsibility for the assignment He has given. He delights to have us roll back on Him the whole responsibility instead of attempting to carry it on our own. He longs for you in fact to relinquish to Him the government of your life and the work He has given to you. Let it be indeed upon His shoulders, if you would experience the increased peace and rest which He promises.

> For unto us a child is born, unto us a son is given: and the government shall be upon his shoulder . . . . Of the increase of his government and peace there shall be no end . . . .
>
> Isaiah 9:6, 7

GOD HAS SAID

"Ye have not chosen me, but I have
chosen you, and ordained you,
that ye should go and bring forth fruit,
and that your fruit should remain"
(John 15:16).

THEREFORE I MAY BOLDLY SAY

I am
God's
responsibility.

He will give the words and the message as th
sion demands it, and He will assume the respon
to see that His purposes are accomplished. As we know
the calling is from Him, so can we be sure that He will
bring forth the fruit—the results.

> Ye have not chosen me, but I have chosen you, and
> ordained you, that ye should go and bring forth fruit, and
> that your fruit should remain: that whatsoever ye shall ask
> of the Father in my name, he may give it you.
>
> John 15:16

He assumes the responsibility for the response of
those to whom I go to minister. He ". . . confirmeth the
word of his servant, and performeth the counsel of his
messengers . . ." (Isaiah 44:26).

> So shall my word be that goeth forth out of my mouth: it
> shall not return unto me void, but it shall accomplish that
> which I please, and it shall prosper in the thing whereto I
> sent it.
>
> Isaiah 55:11

God assumes full responsibility to give direction and
leadership to the one committed to Him.

> I will instruct thee and teach thee in the way which
> thou shalt go: I will guide thee with mine eye.
>
> Psalms 32:8

> . . . I am the Lord thy God which teacheth thee to
> profit, which leadeth thee by the way that thou shouldest
> go.
>
> Isaiah 48:17

God assumes the responsibility of quieting the enemy
of our soul.

. . . When the enemy shall come in like a flood, the
Spirit of the Lord shall lift up a standard against him.

Isaiah 59:19

No weapon that is formed against thee shall prosper;
and every tongue that shall rise against thee in judgment
thou shalt condemn. This is the heritage of the servants of
the Lord, and their righteousness is of me, saith the Lord.

Isaiah 54:17

He assumes full responsibility to give satisfaction and
refresh the one who comes to Him.

. . . And My people shall be satisfied with My goodness . . . . For I satisfy the weary ones and refresh every
one who languishes.

Jeremiah 31:14, 25 NAS

God assumes full responsibility for the one who is
entirely His—wedded not to his own viewpoint, but
God's; involved not in his own enterprises, but God's;
seeking not his own glory, but God's; operating not from
his own individual standpoint, but God's.

*Father, thank You that You are ready to assume fully
the responsibility for me. Thank You for giving me the
privilege of belonging to You entirely. I want to be entirely Yours—totally committed to You and Your will
for my life—with no reserves. Help me to fully cooperate with You, truly believe Your promises, and enjoy the
peace and rest which You desire to give me in every
situation and circumstance. Thank You for assuming
responsibility for my needs as a person and in my assignments for You. In Jesus' name,* amen.

Turning Insight into Action

1. Expand Your Understanding

Look back through the chapter and write down the condition on which God assumes responsibility for His child. List specific areas and situations in which God assumes responsibility for you. Study these verses: Isaiah 43:1, 3; 46:3, 4; Jeremiah 18:1–6; John 15:16.

2. Search and Share

Think back through your past experiences and recall times when it was evident to you that the Lord assumed responsibility for you—did not allow you to be tempted more than you could bear, wonderfully provided for you in the midst of a need, supernaturally enabled you to fulfill an assignment, worked good out of a very difficult and trying situation, gave direction and leadership, or kept you safe, as He did this one:

> I had a real experience this week where I knew God was watching over me. All day I was driving around in the car—down hills, stopping quickly at stop signs, going around sharp corners—but just as I slowed down to turn in our own driveway, I didn't have any brakes. God took me safely home, and there He showed me what was wrong. What a loving Father to care for me in this way!

Write out one or two examples of your experiences. Include any Scripture which was especially meaningful to you. Share with your friends.

3. Develop Your Awareness

Using the list that you made under "Expand Your Understanding," have a session of thanks to God each morning. Thank Him for every area in which He has assumed responsibility for your life. Add to your list during the week as you become aware of other areas where He is responsible for you.

Check up on your own growth in worth. You will be encouraged as you note specific areas of improvement as one friend shared with me:

> I know I've made some progress, because I no longer feel guilty over doing things for myself. Instead, I now have a warm feeling when looking for a new pair of sunglasses for myself or simply sitting down by myself to read for a while. When I goof (like burning the vegetables), or when I say the wrong thing in the wrong way, I don't go to pieces and get angry with myself. I try to decide how I could have done it better and also make things right, if I can. Most of all, I don't run myself down anymore. It's great to see God working, giving me confidence in Him that He did well on this piece of His creation!

4. Store Up God's Thoughts

"Ye have not chosen me, but I have chosen you, and ordained you, that ye should go and bring forth fruit, and that your fruit should remain . . ." (John 15:16).

Additional verses for memory—Isaiah 43:3, 4; Philippians 1:6; Romans 8:28; 1 Corinthians 10:13; Psalms 32:8.

5. Reach Out in Love

(a) Because of your own weakness or infirmity in a certain area you may be especially sensitive to another's need or feeling—one who is lonely, discouraged, feeling inferior, feeling useless. Pray specifically for that person that he will realize that God has assumed responsibility for that problem and will find that God's all-sufficient grace is for him too. Ask the Lord for an opportunity to encourage him through your words or actions.

(b) Together with someone else, study the lives of one or more of the following Bible characters to see how God assumed responsibility for them in the areas mentioned in this chapter.

Abraham	Naomi
Noah	Esther
Ruth	

(c) Take a fruit plate to a widow, a person who lives alone, or a family. Include a note of appreciation for that person, or persons. Using a colored plate or colored tissue paper or cellophane or a colored ribbon can add attractiveness. Any variety of fruits such as apples, pears, oranges, grapes is appropriate—whatever is in season.

(d) Write a letter to a family member or friend expressing your appreciation for the way he has especially influenced your life for God. Mention specific things such as his godly example of patience, generosity, joy, or thankfulness.

6. Sing the Truth

Since I'm now committed to Him,
He's responsible for me.
I am under His protection,
Object of His constant care.
How I praise Him, how I praise Him,
For His constant, loving care,
For His constant, loving care.

13
You Are Under God's Constant Care

It is a comforting, restful thought to know that our loving Heavenly Father has given us the gracious invitation to cast all our care upon Him, because He cares for us (*see* 1 Peter 5:7). The Amplified Bible puts it this way:

Casting the whole of your care—all your anxieties, all your worries, all your concerns, once and for all—on Him; for He cares for you affectionately, and cares about you watchfully.

Though I said this is a gracious *invitation*, it is actually more; it is a gracious *command*. It is out of God's great desire that His children experience full joy and peace that He gives this command. It is the unchanging, everloving, almighty, merciful Heavenly Father who gives this command. How He longs for us to roll the whole weight of our care upon Him, confident that He cares. Oh, what a blessed privilege it is to have Him care for us—the God of the universe, caring about my feelings, my needs, my concerns!

Let not your heart be troubled: ye believe in God, believe also in me.
                                                    John 14:1

Surely goodness and mercy shall follow me all the days of my life . . . .
                                                    Psalms 23:6

Bright Days, Anxious Days

God's goodness and God's unfailing kindness go with me all the days of my life! "All the days"—from birth to death—means all kinds of days—dark days, brighter days, dreary days, anxious days, trying days. Today, all day, in the midst of your special circumstances, know assuredly that God's goodness is yours for today. His mercy is yours for today; His unfailing love—yours for today! Draw near to Him and draw upon these precious, adequate, peace-producing resources! Today! God is here. He cares. And His grace is still all-sufficient. ". . . the Lord God, even my God . . . will not fail thee, nor forsake thee . . ." (1 Chronicles 28:20).

There is not a moment when His thoughts are not on you, when His eye is not focused on you, or when His personal interest is not directed toward you. His great, personal care for you never falters! He is the unchanging One. He is never weary of helping you, strengthening you in your weaknesses, or even forgiving your sins. With loving understanding He is continually aware of you.

> Hast thou not known? hast thou not heard, that the everlasting God, the Lord, the Creator of the ends of the earth, fainteth not, neither is weary? there is no searching of his understanding.
>
> Isaiah 40:28

This God is my Father. He will not fail or forsake me. He will never forget me, nor will His power ever be exhausted so that He cannot provide my needs. It is because we don't call upon Him that we remain unhelped. Let us come boldly and find grace to help in time of need.

In a sense God searches for opportunities to help His children.

> For the eyes of the Lord run to and fro throughout the whole earth, to shew himself strong in the behalf of them whose heart is perfect toward him . . . .
>
> 2 Chronicles 16:9

We often complain that we have no help—and all the while the eyes of the Lord are looking compassionately and longingly at us. He knows the sorrow, trial, or temptation. Nothing would give Him greater pleasure than to show Himself strong on our behalf.

Cast Your Care

When overcome with failure and sin, when thoroughly discouraged, when overtaken suddenly by temptation, you need to know that even this "care" can be cast upon Him. Believe that He forgives and cleanses and continues to care. Nothing will surprise Him or wear out His patience or nullify His love. He is committed to us—He is our God; we are His people.

He delights for us to talk to Him about every "little" thing which concerns us. He is very interested in the things that you are interested in—the things which bring you joy, the things which bring you sorrow. He wants you to share with Him your feelings about your weaknesses. He is touched with the feeling of your infirmity (*see* Hebrews 4:15). He understands, He loves, and He cares. He wants so much for you to know how much He cares and desires to help you in the time of your need, but He waits for you to come to Him. He wants you to give Him another opportunity to show you what He is really like—how much He understands, how much He cares. He waits, that He might be gracious to you (*see* Isaiah 30:18). Many times we grieve Him by not coming to Him, sharing our need with Him, and trusting Him to help us. We limit Him by not letting Him prove to us afresh how much He cares.

Our loving Heavenly Father wants us to cast on Him the cares of our inner person, the struggles with our feelings. He cares about that which causes us distress. He cares about how we feel when others misunderstand or mistreat us. When our hearts are heavy with sorrow or grief and are almost breaking, He cares. He cares when the body may be wracked with pain or when we feel rejected by those we dearly love. He understands, He loves, He cares. He invites you to come to Him and let Him show you that He cares.

Come unto me, all ye that labour and are heavy laden, and I will give you rest.

Matthew 11:28

. . . In returning and rest shall ye be saved; in quietness and in confidence shall be your strength . . . .

Isaiah 30:15

Inner Fears

He cares about the fears you have—the inner fears you don't really want to share with anyone. He wants you to come to Him and let Him dispel those fears.

The Lord is my light and my salvation; whom shall I fear? the Lord is the strength of my life; of whom shall I be afraid?

Psalms 27:1

What time I am afraid, I will trust in thee. In God I will praise his word, in God I have put my trust; I will not fear what flesh can do unto me . . . In God have I put my trust: I will not be afraid what man can do unto me.

Psalms 56:3, 4, 11

Our Lord invites us to come to Him and take shelter under His loving, caring, protecting wings.

. . . The beloved of the Lord shall dwell in safety by him; and the Lord shall cover him all the day long, and he shall dwell between his shoulders.

Deuteronomy 33:12

I am under His protection. Protection from enemies without and enemies within. As I am yielded to Him and trusting in Him, He will protect me from making wrong decisions of major consequence. He will give me discerning judgment when others might wrongly take advantage of me. He will keep me from being seriously distracted from my basic commitment to Him.

God is my Refuge, my Strength, my Counselor, my Guide, my Wisdom, my Fortress, my Protection from the evil that could otherwise overtake me (*see* Psalms 9:9; 18:2). Oh, how comforting to know He is constantly thinking of me, loving me, protecting me, caring for me.

Thank You, Blessed Lord, that You care about everything that touches me. Thank You that You want me to cast all my anxieties, my concerns, on You and experience how much You really care for me. Thank You that You never forget about me nor will ever forsake me. Help me to refuse to carry any care myself and always come under the shelter of Your loving, caring, protect-

GOD HAS SAID

"Casting all your care upon him;
for he careth for you"
(1 Peter 5:7).

THEREFORE I MAY BOLDLY SAY

*I am
under God's
constant care.*

ing wings. Thank You for Your constant, loving care. In Jesus' name, amen.

Turning Insight Into Action

1. Expand Your Understanding

Review the chapter and jot down several statements that indicate what God says about how much He cares about you. Which verse and thought is especially meaningful to you? Why?

Study briefly the life of Joseph from Genesis 37–50, especially noticing how God cared for him in the varying and difficult circumstances of his life. Remember, this is an illustration of how much He cares for you, how faithful He will be to you.

2. Search and Share

Shortly after my husband's death I went to visit my sister and brother-in-law. The whole first night I spent lying awake worrying about how we were going to live with no income. As I shared some of my worrying the next morning, my brother-in-law quietly asked me if I had forgotten about God. His gentle suggestion was the prod I needed to roll the whole burden on my Heavenly Father and trust Him to care for us. When I went back to my own home, I needed $290.00 to pay the rent, phone, and car payment. In the next few days I received checks in the mail from relatives who had no idea of my need. They totaled $288.00—and I had $2.00 cash on hand! Since then God has supplied even greater needs—new friends, a job. And He has filled the void of emptiness and loneliness. How well I know I am under God's constant, loving care!

Think through some of your past experiences and review God's faithfulness in caring for you. Write out three statements or brief illustrations showing how He cared for you. It would be good to let this become a habit—keeping a record of God's faithful, loving care throughout your life.

3. Develop Your Awareness

This week as you memorize verses speaking of God's care for you, notice how He does this for you. Jot down notes on His faithfulness. Let your heart ring with praise and thanksgiving for what He has done, is now doing, and with hope in your heart for what He shall continue to be and to do for you.

4. Store Up God's Thoughts

"Casting all your care upon him; for he careth for you" (1 Peter 5:7).

Additional memory verses—1 Chronicles 28:20; 2 Chronicles 16:9; Deuteronomy 33:12; Matthew 11:28.

5. Reach Out in Love

One of the best ways to demonstrate to others that God cares for them is to show that *you* care for them. Also one of the best ways to thank God for His care for you (other than to tell Him in words), is to care for others in His name. ". . . Inasmuch as ye have done it unto one of the least of these . . . ye have done it unto me" (Matthew 25:40). This week communicate your care for another in these ways:

(a) Visit a sick one. You might take some flowers or a card. Before you go, call and offer to bring them something they might need from your home or from a store.

(b) Visit an elderly person who is alone or in a rest home. Take this one some type of food you know they enjoy—a small rice pudding, some nuts, homemade bread, and so forth.

(c) Plan for some special way to help each member of your family this week, such as: helping with kitchen cleanup, reading a story to a young child, baking some cookies, polishing shoes, raking leaves or mowing the lawn, helping a brother or sister with a project or homework, buying an ice-cream cone for brother or sister.

6. Sing the Truth

> Since I'm now committed to Him,
> He's responsible for me.
> I am under His protection,
> Object of His constant care.
> How I praise Him, how I praise Him,
> For His constant, loving care,
> For His constant, loving care.
>
> I am God's own special treasure,
> One who's precious in His sight.
> He has set His love upon me
> And in Him my soul delights.
> Oh, what wonder, how amazing!
> He has set His love on me,
> He has set His love on me.

A personal growth guide for individual response and group study is available directly from the Enriched Living Workshop, P.O. Box 3039, Kent, WA 98031.

Reading Notes

1. J. I. Packer, *Knowing God* (Downers Grove, Illinois: InterVarsity Press, 1973), p. 184.
2. F. B. Meyer, *Great Verses Through the Bible* (Grand Rapids, Michigan: Zondervan, 1966), p. 459.
3. Ibid., p. 397.
4. Oswald Chambers, *My Utmost for His Highest: The Golden Book of Oswald Chambers* (New York: Dodd, Mead and Company, 1935), p. 265.
5. F. B. Meyer, *Great Verses Through the Bible* (Grand Rapids, Michigan: Zondervan, 1966), pp. 284–285.